Reunited

Reunited

• • •

*An Investigative Genealogist
Unlocks Some of Life's Greatest
Family Mysteries*

• • •

PAMELA SLATON

with SAMANTHA MARSHALL

3 1336 08987 1280

🦁 St. Martin's Griffin 🐾 New York

REUNITED. Copyright © 2012 by Pamela Slaton. All rights reserved. Printed in the United States of America. For information, address St. Martin's Press, 175 Fifth Avenue, New York, N.Y. 10010.

www.stmartins.com

Design by Gretchen Achilles

LIBRARY OF CONGRESS CATALOGING-IN-PUBLICATION DATA

Slaton, Pamela.
    Reunited : an investigative genealogist unlocks some of life's greatest family mysteries / Pamela Slaton; with Samantha Marshall. — 1st ed.
        p. cm.
    ISBN 978-0-312-61732-5 (trade pbk.)
    ISBN 978-1-250-01213-5 (e-book)
    1. Birthparents—United States—Identification—Case studies.
    2. Adoptees—United States—Identification—Case studies.   I. Title.
    HV875.55.S615 2012
    362.82'98—dc23

                                                    2012004630

First Edition: May 2012

10 9 8 7 6 5 4 3 2 1

I write this to honor the memory of the Monaci family—my family.

Contents

◆ ◆ ◆

Author's Note

. . .

As I think about how I ended up in this crazy place I find myself in today, it's only natural to think of the people who have inspired and shaped my life from the very beginning. I can remember always feeling loved and special, even before I could crawl. I was consistently aware of the existence of my birth mother and the fact that she gave birth to me, but at the same time I adored my adoptive parents. There was no question that the mother and father who raised me were my real parents.

Still, I searched for what I believed to be the perfect fantasy mother. I found her, and to say that she fell short of this ideal is an understatement.

My mother (my true mother), Ann, was a strong-willed, no-nonsense kind of woman who had endured many great losses during her lifetime. Her father and mother were both deceased by the time she was twenty-nine years old. But that was just the beginning of her heartbreak. My brother, Ronnie, a very young man, displayed a courage that was inexplicable. He knew that he was losing his battle with his cancer and desperately tried to hide his increasingly frightening symptoms from my parents. Sadly, my brother lost his fight to this horrible disease in May 1984, at the age of twenty-two. Looking back, I don't know how my parents survived the unbearable grief of losing a child.

Then my dad, Ronald, passed away at the tragically young age of fifty-four. I knew that he would not live to be an old man. When I prayed at night, I would beg God to let him live long enough to meet his grandchild, to help him heal the hole in his heart from the loss of my brother. At the very least, I wanted to be able to tell him I was expecting before he died. I learned I was pregnant with my first son on October 20, 1988. Dad was overjoyed with the news and bragged to anyone who would listen that he was going to be a grandfather. Then my father, my first love, died on October 24, 1988, a mere four days after learning the news of my pregnancy. God did answer my prayer. We buried him with the picture of my son's first sonogram. Eight months later, my baby was born. Ronald Slaton entered the world at a whopping ten pounds, two ounces. My boy Ronnie was the light that we needed in our lives. I can't help but wonder if Dad had a hand in helping to whip up this supersized baby from Heaven above.

I gave birth to my second son, Mikey ("Mo Mo"), in 1994. Although not as large a baby as his brother, he made sure we all knew he was present. As a little guy, he was a character, and remains so today.

Mom came to live with us in South Jersey in 2002. She loved to cook and do laundry. I was not going to argue. My business keeps me busy ten hours or more a day and her help was a Godsend. Her presence was just the kind of inspiration our little family needed. At my mom's insistence, we all gathered around our kitchen table at 5:00 P.M. every night to have dinner and enjoy her incredible home cooking, just as we had during my childhood.

I experienced a great loss in September 2010. My mom, after having minor surgery, which should have been free of complications, suffered a blood clot and was gone in an instant. She died in my house, with my arms around her. I cannot express how great a loss this is to me. My mother, my best friend, my rock, and the last surviving member of my immediate family, was gone. She left me to join Dad and Ronnie in Heaven. She'd long told me she was ready to go, but I just hadn't expected it to be quite so soon.

The pain is still raw. For the first time in my life, I really do feel like an orphan. I have experienced a deep sense of anger, sadness, and abandonment—a depth of despair that I never knew existed. I also realize that everything I thought I was searching for was right under my nose the whole time.

My mother's courage and strength never dimmed, and I am inspired by her daily in everything that I do.

I am who I am because of the family who raised me and the love of my husband, Mike, who is a gift from God, as well as the blessings of my two boys.

As an adoptee who does family searches for a living, I have always believed that DNA is a vital part of what we are. But ultimately, it is how we love, respect, and nurture one another that make us *who* we are. This is what my real family, my adoptive family, has taught me.

Introduction

◆ ◆ ◆

People always ask me why so many adoptees feel the urge to search. Even when our childhoods are perfect, with wonderful adoptive parents and tight-knit, nurturing families, the desire to know is always there, lurking under the surface. We can't escape it.

I'll tell you why we search, and it isn't necessarily for the reasons you might think. In the decade and a half since I first started in the search business, I've solved more than three thousand cases, and for almost every single one of my clients, it's not a matter of replacing an existing family. They don't expect to find some love they never had. It's not some selfish quest for more affection. It's about acknowledgment. It's about being able to say to your birth mother, *I'm okay. I had a good life. You did the right thing. I hope you moved on with your life. I hope you're okay, too.*

Searching for one's origins means nothing less than validating one's own existence. Everyone wants to know where they came from. It's a subject that eternally fascinates. Most people take their origins for granted. For the nonadopted, the basic parameters are obvious. They know where they got those dimples, the color of their eyes, their curly hair or straight hair, their medical history. But for adoptees, their lineage is represented by a big black void. At some point in their lives, the desire to know is going to hit hard. As I tell my clients, "You weren't dropped off from the mother ship. You are someone, and you came from somewhere."

These are the stories of adoptees and their search for themselves. The impulse to search is about the basic human need to connect with those who gave you life. At a minimum, it offers closure. It fills in the missing pages in the story of our lives. We need to know that first chapter to better understand ourselves and what happens next. Beyond that, the search teaches us something profound about humanity and the blood ties that bind despite decades of separation.

Believe me, this is not another advocacy book pushing the open adoption agenda. Sure, I bump up against plenty of the laws and bureaucratic obstacles that make my job more difficult, but I keep pounding until I get past them. More than 90 percent of the time, I solve the case I'm working on. Along the way, I'll stumble into dead ends and get sidetracked by countless false leads. But that's just part of the journey. Each blind alley and miscue teaches me something fascinating about the process of the search and the hope and disappointment it brings. With every case, I feel like a character in an emotionally charged suspense novel. I get a little lost in their stories as I seek to reunite adoptees with their birth parents across all walks of life. For me, it's personal. Each successful case helps bring back some of the missing pieces in my own failed attempt to reunite with my birth mother. I get to be a part of some of the most moving and gratifying moments in my clients' lives, and each time I get to bear witness, it heals me just a little bit.

And every journey I go on with the sons, daughters, mothers, and fathers who are searching teaches me something. I've learned, for instance, that you can separate two siblings and cast them to opposite sides of the world, but their personality traits and life paths can be so similar, it's as if they're one. That's how strong the blood bond can be. I've learned that most mothers and fathers never forget the children they lost, even when they've lived nearly a century and had many other children, grandchildren, and great-grandchildren in the interim. Most of the time, birth parents want to be found, and these families open up their lives to one another.

I'll take you on these journeys with me. Over the following pages, you'll read about my most memorable clients, from the Alabama mother who never forgot the baby who was taken from her when she had her at fourteen, to the retired factory worker who found his mom right before she died, at ninety-three. She was waiting for him all along. I'll take you into their lives and let you in on a few of my trade secrets along the way. I've cherry-picked through stacks of case files to share with you some of my most startling and moving cases. The pain of separation for many of these grown-up children is palpable.

One of those kids was Rapper Darryl "DMC" McDaniels of Run–DMC. He had all the fame and success anyone could dream of, but he was still haunted by the mystery of his past. At thirty-five, as he began work on his autobiography, he asked his mother for more information about his family, and it was only then that she shared with him that he'd been adopted. This led to the making of an Emmy Award–winning documentary, *My Adoption Journey*. What followed was a tumultuous ride that led him from support group to support group. He could barely contain his anger and frustration when he learned that his birth certificate would be forever sealed, as is often the case in a closed adoption. Then he found me, and I made the connection he'd been longing for for most of his adult life. He now says finding his roots helped him heal a wound he never knew he had: "It wasn't just about finding my birth parents," he told me. "It was about finding myself."

Many reunions are bittersweet. Take, for example, the story of a woman in Pennsylvania. When she gave birth to her daughter, the midwives told her the baby had died. It was a way of saving the Mennonite family's reputation, because the child was born out of wedlock, and preventing the anguished mother from resisting the adoption process. Mother and child were reunited fifty-five years later. They'd missed out on a lifetime together—a situation that the mother would have never chosen herself. I don't care how old you are. When you are an adopted child, the desire to know can last a lifetime. And when you are a birth parent, that knowledge is always with you. You never forget.

There are about five million adoptees living in the United States today, yet open adoptions still haven't been widely embraced in this country, shrouding the past in mystery for many thousands of seekers. Yet the desire to know is inescapable. The need to find one's roots is primal. For many adoptees, it's not about replacing the families who raised them. It's about reconnecting to a generations-long lineage and understanding their own DNA. Without that knowledge, their past will always seem like unfinished business. It's my mission to provide these men and women with what they need to know about themselves. I help them complete their own circle so they can finally move forward with their lives.

Over 60 percent of Americans are affected by adoption in some way. Their fundamentally human journeys reveal something about us as sons, daughters, brothers, sisters, mothers, and fathers. Each chapter in this book details a heroic quest for self-knowledge, love, and healing. The personal histories of these brave individuals will have universal appeal that resonates far beyond the adoptee population. Because we all need to know who we are, and what brought us here. These powerful tales of the lost and found will help readers appreciate their own history, and inspire us to discover more about those who came before us, and our place in the story of humanity.

Although I did not get the reunion of my fantasies, I've had the privilege of being part of something much, much bigger. Somehow, some way, we are all connected. Through the years, I've also reunited long-lost friends, war buddies, and many others who endured forced separations due to circumstances beyond their control. Such an experience stays with you. Readers will learn how the unanswered question "Whatever happened to . . ." can haunt someone for decades. No one lives in a vacuum. In a sense, we are all adoptees seeking our identity and place within the human family. We all need to belong.

TO SEARCH OR NOT TO SEARCH?

That is one of the biggest questions adoptees can ask themselves, and it plagues most of us our whole lives. Searching is not for everyone. Of course I encounter people who do not wish to be found, or who do not even want to start a search. They tell me, "*If it ain't broke, don't fix it*" or "*Don't upset the applecart.*" But those aren't the real reasons. Something much more fundamental is going on. Fear of the unknown is far greater than the truth.

It always saddens me to learn that people will not start a search because they are afraid of intruding on the other person's life. Most of the time, the other person is also not reaching out for the same reason. So much time is lost in this pointless holding pattern. I often have to remind clients who are hesitant to reach out to their birth families for fear of shocking them that their families already know they had this child. The shock is simply that they have been found. In today's information age, with all the things that can be uncovered through the Internet, it always amazes me when people do not expect to be located.

Ultimately, once adoptees reach out to the other person, they are often surprised to learn that they are welcome. The vast majority of the cases I handle end up going well. By "well" I mean that, at a minimum, both parties receive the closure of knowing their answers. They get to reach out and say simply, "*I never forgot you,*" or "*Here is vital medical information.*" An ongoing relationship is a bonus by far.

The other obstacle people face in their search is the loyalty issue. Many adoptees believe that if they want to meet their birth mothers or fathers, or any other blood relatives, it will be perceived as an indication that their adoptive family wasn't enough, and that they somehow need or want more. So many adoptees are afraid of hurting their adoptive parents. They live in fear that if they choose to meet their birth family, they will make the ones they love most—the people who raised them—feel inadequate or threatened.

The adoptive family can't help but be aware that their child is linked by DNA to another family. They need to understand how crucial it is to be supportive of the adopted child. Blood ties are a part of who we are, and a need to know one's beginnings should be expected. You cannot underestimate the impact of DNA. The unconscious power of our genetic heritage is nothing short of miraculous.

However, the need for support goes both ways. This is sensitive stuff, and it makes everyone involved feel vulnerable and raw. Our parents are only human, and feelings aren't dictated by logic or facts. I personally witnessed my own mother's insecurity when she felt a meeting with my birth mother was imminent. I had to reassure her that nothing could ever change my love for her. She was in fact my *real* mother, the woman who raised me and nurtured me during my whole life, and there was no one who could ever change that. But it begs the question: If a parent can love more than one child, why can't a child love more than one parent?

My good friend DMC said it best when he described his birth mother and his adoptive mother as a "unity of motherhood." He does not view his birth mother and adoptive mother as separate entities. His heart is large enough that he can love them both, and the fact that he could love his birth mother does not in any way take away from his love for the mother who brought him into her home. If anything, he appreciates both women all the more. The fact remains that for adoptees, it takes two. Our natural mother gave us life. Our adoptive parents gave us a nurturing and loving home. They gave us our family.

It is a basic human desire to want to know where you came from, who you look like, and your medical background. It is also pure parental instinct for a birth mother or father to want to know that the baby they surrendered is alive and well. They naturally need to know that their sacrifice in giving up their son or daughter resulted in a better life for their child.

Life is too short and too precious to live with these nagging questions. If you have ever dreamed of knowing the truth, do not let fear stand in your way. You may miss the opportunity of a lifetime.

The stories you will read on the following pages teach us what it means to love and care for someone we've never even met. Searching for a lost child or parent takes tremendous courage and strength, but the rewards are immense. This kind of search transforms lives. In the thousands of cases I've worked on, I've gotten a front row seat to witness the extraordinary power and capacity of the human heart, and it floors me every time. So this isn't just a book about a few lost souls and what they found. This is the story of humanity, and of the hope that lies in everyone's search.

Reunited

CHAPTER ONE

A Searcher Is Born

◆ ◆ ◆

It was a conversation I'd been waiting to have my whole life. For my thirtieth birthday, my husband, Mike, hired a private investigator, and in five days this man did what I hadn't been able to do in fourteen years. He found my birth mother. I finally had a name, a number, and an address for this elusive woman. There was no doubt.

When Mike called me from work with the contact details, he made me promise not to call until he got home. He should have known better. "Yeah, yeah, sure, babe, don't worry. I promise I'll wait," I told him, my fingers itching to start dialing as soon as I got him off the phone. My heart was racing. Meanwhile, my mother-in-law was hovering. She knew what I was up to and she had a bad feeling.

"Why don't you look happy for me?" I asked her.

"Because I'm worried; I don't want to see you get hurt."

"It'll be fine. If she's anything like me, she'll be thrilled to get this call."

I picked up the phone and dialed, but the person who answered—presumably my half brother—told me she was at the supermarket. I tried again later and got my half sister, who told me she was still out. I was on tenterhooks. I couldn't get over the fact that I had a brother and sister, and I'd just talked to them for the first time, although they had no idea who I was.

I waited for another interminable hour. Finally, on my third try, my birth mother answered the phone. We'll call her Priscilla.

"Yeah? Who is this?"

"Hello, Priscilla. My name is Pamela Slaton. I was born on February 23, 1964, under the name of Wade, then given up for adoption. I recently found out that I am your daughter."

"No, you're not. And you should never have called me!"

"Yes, I am. I have documented proof that you are my birth mother. It's true."

"Oh no, I'm not!"

"Oh yes, you are!"

"No! I am NOT!"

This back-and-forth continued for a while. Priscilla was tough. She grew up in the Bronx and had that thick accent of the streets. But I grew up in Queens and could be just as tough. Not that I felt strong. It was really just my defense mechanism kicking in. The last thing I expected was to be denied by my own flesh and blood, and I was stunned. So I resorted to being a wiseass.

"Listen, Priscilla, we can do this now, over the phone, or I can get in my car and be on your doorstep in three hours. Which would you prefer?"

"You just stay away from me, you hear? Okay, yeah, I may be your biological mother, but I never cared about you or gave you a second thought in all these years. I don't know what you want from me."

"You know what, Priscilla? It's cool. It's fine. Just tell me who my father is and I'll go away."

"You want to know who your father is? Sure, I'll tell you who your father is. Your father was my father. I hope you enjoy knowing that."

Then she slammed down the phone, and my whole world turned upside down. I never saw it coming. I'd been so sure Priscilla would be overjoyed to hear from me. Instead, I felt like I'd had my teeth kicked out. The room was spinning and I literally saw black and white dots, as if the cable had gone out on an old TV set in my head. The woman I'd been searching for and dreamed of meeting ever since I could remember had flung this horrifying information at me as if it were a poison dart, and her aim was dead-on. It pierced right through my chest.

The next day, I was scheduled to have gallbladder surgery. Like an idiot, I went through with it. The doctors expected me to be out of recovery in an hour, but it took seven hours. They couldn't lower my heart rate. Every time I came to, I'd remember the conversation from the night before and get slammed with an anxiety attack. A nurse came out of the waiting room and told my husband she was concerned that my vital signs still weren't stable. She asked him if I'd been traumatized in any way recently, and he told her what had happened.

"Well, that would do it," she said.

Obviously, I survived. But now I understand what people mean when they say you can literally die of a broken heart. I almost did.

CHILDHOOD FANTASY

I was about three years old when I first thought about searching for my birth mother. Becoming a searcher for adoptees and their birth relatives is something I was born to do. My aunt has told me she remembers that I said, "I am going to find that woman." I kept saying it over and over. She asked me, "What woman?" Then it dawned on her who I meant.

I never discussed this with my parents. Even as a child, I instinctively knew it would hurt them. My desire to find my birth mother was in no way intended to be a slight against my mother and father. No blood relation could ever replace the people who loved me and raised me. I was brought into a loving middle-class home in the suburbs. My dad was a funeral director and my mother was a stay-at-home mom. I had an older brother, who was also adopted. If anything, we were made to feel even more special that we had been "chosen." Because of the positive way my parents framed it for me, I was actually proud of the fact I was adopted. My poor mom was mortified when, as a toddler, I'd blurt out this fact of my existence to any random person who came within earshot. I was adopted and proud of it.

Don't misunderstand me. It's always been very clear in my mind that the Monaci family, who raised me, is my real family. I was brought up by the most incredible, loving, wonderful parents. None of us was tied by blood, but that didn't matter. Love, loyalty, and honesty were our bond, and it was much bigger than sharing someone's DNA.

My mom married my father, Ron, at nineteen. My dad suffered many illnesses during their marriage. They could not have biological children because, as a young child, my father had suffered a devastating injury that forced him to undergo repeated exposure to radiation. All those X-rays made him sterile. Dad actually had undiagnosed lupus and spent most of his life suffering from the many side effects of this disease. When I was five years old, a blood clot almost took his life, and I remember a feeling of overwhelming terror at the thought of losing this great man. As if seeing my father suffer from one health crisis after another was not enough, my brother, Ronnie, was diagnosed with bone cancer at the tender age of nineteen. My mother was a soldier at my brother's side as she struggled to do whatever possible to nurture him back to health. We supported each other through the greatest of hardships, and we survived them together.

I learned from my parents the true meaning of family as we sat down to a dinner that my mom had on the table by 5:00 P.M. sharp every evening. It was our chance to talk about our day and just check in with the people who cared about us the most. I felt secure and safe. My parents were best friends who helped each other through every obstacle in their lives. My brother and I were raised in a God-fearing family and were sent to private school for our early education. We went to church every Sunday and arrived home to await the arrival of our grandparents (my dad's parents), who were Italian and brought with them all of my favorite foods—meatballs, manicotti, cannoli. I gain weight just thinking about it! Our extended family dined together every Sunday. Our grandmother smothered us with kisses (we called her "the Octopus"), and our grandfather, who chain-smoked Lucky Strike cigarettes, squeezed our noses with his tobacco-stained fingers. These were good, hardworking people who taught me the meaning of the word *integrity* and gave me all the unconditional love I could ever have asked for. It was a great foundation.

But this yearning to find the woman who gave me life was so fundamental that I couldn't switch it off. I think this is true for most adoptees. Think of all those millions of people who are fascinated with their family ancestry, and then multiply that obsession by a factor of a thousand. It's something primal. There's so much that our immediate blood relatives can tell us about ourselves. This need to connect is especially intense when it comes to our birth mothers. It's an organic bond that's always there. You were in this person's womb. No matter what happens, you are her flesh and blood, and it will always feel like a piece of you is missing without her acknowledgment.

That feeling stays close to the surface your whole life. In school, I always wanted to be a writer, and when I was fifteen, I wrote a haiku that went something like this:

THE RING

It sat glistening at the bottom of the ocean
Forever lost

Cast away uncaringly
As he cast away her

Of course, it was about my birth parents, or how I'd imagined them to be. You create so many scenarios in your head about what happened and the circumstances that led to your being given up for adoption. Until you know the real answers, it never stops.

THE FIRST STEP

At sixteen, my best friend took me into Manhattan to visit the agency that had handled my adoption, Spence-Chapin. She bought me a teddy bear at Lord & Taylor, we had lunch, and then we went to the place where it all began. I was turned away almost immediately and told to come back when I was eighteen. But I stayed in the lobby for a few minutes to take it all in—the furniture, the shabby wallpaper, everything. There was something almost mystical about that spot, because I knew it was the last place I'd been with my birth mother, and the first location where I met my parents. Of course, I had been just a baby at the time, but I tried so hard to remember what it had been like. Being in those offices just fueled my desire to learn even more, and the minute I turned eighteen, I was back again.

The agency finally gave me what's called "non-identifying information." I learned that my birth mother was young, only sixteen, when she surrendered me for adoption. The agency described her as five eight, with almost model-like good looks. She had blond hair and blue eyes, she was well spoken, and she was clearly in love with the man presumed to be my father. He was described as handsome, twenty years old, very tall—six five—with dark blond hair and green eyes, and of Italian descent. The agency told me my mother had considered herself a foster child because she wasn't raised by her own parents and was separated from her brother and her sister, but she didn't know why. She was young and unable to raise a child on her own, but she seemed reluctant to give me up. The agency severed her legal ties to me only after she failed to show up for two appointments with one of the agency's social workers.

This made me all the more determined to find her. It was no longer about me. I felt sad for my birth mother and I wanted to know that she was okay, and to let her know that I was fine and I'd had a good life. But over the years, I kept getting stonewalled. I'd pick up scraps of information here and there, think the trail was getting hot, then hit a dead end. Few states have embraced open adoptions, which were unheard of at the time I was born. People in a position to tell me what I needed to know were legally bound not to. All they could do was offer a few murky clues. I finally found out that my birth name was Wade, something my adoptive mother later told me she had known all along, because it was on my adoption papers. (She wasn't exactly supportive of my search. I guess she was afraid I'd get hurt, or that she'd lose me.)

Most adoptees who search go through this stop-and-start process. You pick it up, you put it down, and then you pick it up again. Life and the need to earn a living tend to get in the way. The search can take an emotional toll, and it's all too easy to get obsessive about it, but you can't live like that.

In the interim, I had married my childhood sweetheart, Mike, moved to Nassau County, on Long Island, begun a career in real estate, and started a family. It wasn't until after my father died and my second little guy was born that we had the breakthrough on Priscilla's name and location (and my world came to a crashing halt).

FROM FANTASY TO REALITY

The months following my initial contact with my birth mother were hell. I'd never experienced anxiety before, but that year I went through all the symptoms—insomnia, jitters, depression—on a regular basis. I felt insecure, and I withdrew from my friends and family. One time, I even had a panic attack at the supermarket. The thought that I could be the product of incest made me feel dirty. The idea that a human being could do that to his own child, and that I shared his DNA, shook me to my core. Not to mention my fear for the health of my children. What were the medical complications from incest? I didn't know what this meant.

This spurred me on to search even harder. I decided to fight for my identity and regain a sense of who I was. I knew I had some half brothers and sisters to find, as well as a birth father. When we got home from the hospital after my surgery, one of the first things I did was load our babies into the back of the car and get Mike to drive me to the town where Priscilla had lived her whole life. I remember distinctly that Bon Jovi was blasting on the car stereo, which my husband cranked up to distract me from the pain. My stomach was stapled up from the surgery two days before, but no one could convince me to stay home and rest. When we got to this town, I went immediately to the local library, so that I could look at my half siblings' pictures in their high school yearbooks. I wasn't ready to reach out to them. I couldn't take another rejection. I just needed to see them and know that they existed.

FROM BACK TO FRONT

But first, I had some healing to do. What I didn't know at the time I found Priscilla was that you need to prepare yourself.

People join support groups, read books, and spend years re-searching what can happen before they make that phone call. But I've always had a tendency to dive in headfirst. I did every-thing backward. I joined every adoption organization I could find only after I'd found Priscilla. I needed to find other adop-tees who understood what I was going through. I couldn't stand to be alone in this a minute longer.

I made a ton of new friends. Aside from my brother, Ronnie, who'd had no desire to search when we were growing up, I knew no other adoptees. Suddenly, I was relating to people on a level I never had been able to before. This opened up a whole new world for me. I became instant pals with some women who'd also been searching. We started socializing and had girls' week-ends away in the Hamptons. I was like their social director. They shared their stories with me, and I shared mine with them, and although there were some other disaster stories, no one was able to top what had happened to me.

During this time, I met a woman who threw me a lifeline— I'll call her Lydia. Lydia cofounded a group that ran meetings in various homes and public places. The organization had a 1-800 number and took calls from all over the United States from adoptees and birth parents looking for one another. I found this group within a couple of months of my reunion fiasco and started going to its meetings as well. A mutual friend from the adoption groups introduced me to Lydia, and the friendship was instant.

Lydia was older and wiser than I was in matters of adoption searches, and she immediately took me under her wing. I called her relentlessly to pick her brains about the process of finding birth relatives. We spent hours on the phone. I was looking for my own family and still honing my search skills, and Lydia was generous in opening up her bag of tricks to me. Besides point-ing me to useful resources for information, one of the most valuable lessons she taught me was to trust my gut.

As we got to know each other, I opened up more about my disastrous contact with my birth mother. It wasn't something I necessarily wore on my sleeve—I tend to come across as this outgoing, ballsy woman, but inside I felt fragile. I told Lydia I wanted to find my father, because I needed to know if what Priscilla had said was a lie. Lydia was adamant: "That's total BS, what she told you. There is just no way!"

It was just what I needed to hear. When I told that story to some other adoptees, I could see the pity and embarrassment in their eyes, and that just made me feel worse. But Lydia's indignant reaction came as a relief, and I was inclined to believe her. Lydia had seen these situations play out time and again, and she knew all the signs of denial, guilt, and resentment. Lydia had witnessed dozens of bad reunions over the years, although she admitted mine was probably the worst. She could see my own obstinate nature being reflected back at me tenfold by my birth mother, and she was certain it was another case of someone pushing back hard to make the uncomfortable truth disappear. It was just Priscilla's way of making sure I didn't go poking around in that hornet's nest. Little did she know the child she had given birth to.

THE ROOKIE YEARS

Word among the other adoptees spread that I was getting good at searching on my own behalf, and they started asking me to help them, as well. I soon teamed up with Lydia and another friend, Nanette. Together, we solved some of the toughest adoption cases. It was the most fun I've ever had in my career as a searcher.

On one occasion, we helped Carol—a nice girl from Long Island who knew absolutely nothing about herself, not even her birth name—by trolling the churchyards of the Deep South.

This girl was a riot. We did some searching through the records and learned that she was born Desiree Fender. That wasn't exactly what she was expecting.

"What kind of fucked-up name is that?" she said.

"And we found your father. His name is Rusty!" one of us said, teasing her.

Our search for her birth family took us to a graveyard somewhere in the rural South. For some reason, there were no paper records on the deceased, so I called the church, asking if someone could read off the information on a gravestone, and I got this guy on the phone whom I could barely understand.

"Oh, they done took Junior outta here," the local grave digger told me. "Headstone an' all."

"Huh? Someone robbed the grave?"

"No, ma'am. The family moved out of state and they took Junior with 'em."

Someone had actually dug up his relative's body and loaded it on the back of a pickup truck to relocate it to another churchyard hundreds of miles down the interstate. Apparently, that's how they do it in the South. Lydia and I were in tears, we were laughing so hard. (Luckily, our client shared our warped sense of humor.) We finally located the new resting place and, through Junior, we found a connection to Carol's birth mother. This person was able to tell us that, a few years earlier, Carol's mother had been knocked off her motorcycle and killed in a highway accident. It was sad news, but it gave Carol the answers about her identity she'd been looking for, however bizarre.

One of my favorite search stories from those early years is about a family of bagel makers from Long Island. They'd been looking for their long-lost son for decades. At just seventeen, the parents were kids themselves when they gave up their firstborn. A few years later, they married and started having more kids—a family that was planned this time. But they'd always regretted their earlier decision, even though their circumstances had given them no choice. They put up a plaque over the counter of their bagel shop with their son's birth date, hoping one day he'd walk in and find them. In the reunion of their fantasies, a young man sharing their DNA would walk in and order a dozen sesame and poppy mixed, then recognize his date of birth on the wall and ask its meaning. Of course, it never happened.

As adults, their kids found out about their eldest sibling and spent thousands on specialist searches, but they got nowhere. Then, about fourteen years ago, I met their mother at an adoption support group meeting and she asked if I could help her. (All members of the adoption triad—the birth parents, adoptees, and adoptive parents—show up at these support groups.) One of her sons ended up hiring me, but there was next to no information to work with. It was a private adoption, and with no agency involved, the search became that much harder.

But Lydia had one of her flashes. She calls herself the "Psychic Detective." Sometimes she just pulls information out of the ether. She saw the initials M.S. flash in front of her, and used that to try to find a match among the thousands of names on her database. She narrowed it down to a likely candidate and passed the name on to me. I located the man and spoke to his wife on the phone, who confirmed he was adopted. I managed to convince him to come to Long Island to meet his brother. I still had doubts if this was the right guy, but they vanished the minute this guy walked into the Italian restaurant where we were meeting. My client was convinced. "With a schnoz like that, there's no question he's one of us!" he told me.

GETTING MY CHOPS

Those early years with Lydia and Nanette were the best training a budding searcher could ask for. We were like machines, we cracked so many cases together. Word was starting to spread and we ended up on a popular WKTU radio show out of Jersey City with "Goumba" Johnny and "Hollywood" Hamilton. They had a huge audience of three million listeners in the tristate area, so the pressure was on. People started faxing in their stories, and we were inundated. We had to handpick the cases we could crack at warp speed. It was Valentine's Day and we had to hold live reunions on the four-hour radio-show, broadcast from Manhattan's Tavern on the Green. We ended up solving about a dozen cases in five days, which was unheard of.

Obviously, Lydia taught me well, because my inner voice, along with some old-fashioned sleuthing, was coming in handy. Lydia may think we have some kind of psychic power, but I'm not quite that mystical. Let's just call it good instincts. Then again, there've been moments on this journey that have given me pause and made me wonder if there isn't more to Lydia's brand of spiritualism. About fourteen years ago, Lydia invited a psychic friend of hers from Flushing over to her house on Long Island. We were each allowed to ask her three questions. I didn't really know what to ask her, but she told me I would have a career on television one day. Afterward, I remembered meeting the same woman when I was a teenager, and she had told me the same thing. Maybe she really did see something, because years later I finally did get my show on Oprah's new network. But where I am now all started with my friendship with Lydia, and the lessons she taught me.

OTHER ANGELS

There were many other people who helped me along my path as a searcher, often from some surprising places. I'll be forever grateful to Katherine Boros, a Holocaust survivor who knew she was dying and that her adoption agency was closing. After undergoing dialysis, she dragged herself to her office daily to continue to provide non-identifying information for as many people as she possibly could. Before her death, she contacted several other agencies to let them know that she felt I was ethical and effective at my job and to ask them if they would consider referring me to anyone who needed the services of a professional searcher. Katherine understood firsthand what it was like to lose loved ones and, as a result of her experience, she was sympathetic to those who were searching. She had no one to help her track down her own surviving family members after the war. She taught me that even after enduring her own cruel life experience, she still had limitless reserves of compassion for others.

She was especially helpful in one particular case. Paula Bernstein and Elyse Schein were twin girls born in New York City in 1969. Unknowingly, Bernstein and Schein had been part of a secret research project in the 1960s and 1970s that separated identical twins as infants and followed their development in a one-of-a-kind experiment to assess the influence of nature versus nurture in child development. It was the only study of its kind on twins who had been separated from infancy.

The families had been told they were part of an ongoing study. But neither the parents nor the children knew the real subject of the study—or that the children involved had been separated from their identical twins. They were literally human lab rats. The researchers saw it as the perfect science experiment. If they had kept the twins together, they would have mirrored each other. Separating them was a surefire way of determining whether there really was a natural, genetic tendency for identical twins to dress alike, think alike, and act alike. It was an appalling way of messing with children's lives. This was before 1981, when New York State changed its adoption laws to ensure that siblings would be kept together when they were adopted.

The idea of using human beings in a scientific experiment was too horrifyingly reminiscent of Katherine's past in Nazi Germany. She couldn't live with that knowledge without doing something about it, so she became instrumental in joining Paula and Elyse together by notifying them individually of the fact that each had been born a twin. When Katherine passed away, the adoption community lost a great humanitarian.

I feel privileged to have been a part of these incredible stories. For those of us who search for a living, solving these cases becomes a personal mission. I know that every time I can make a successful reunion happen, there's a level of satisfaction that goes beyond professional pride. It heals me. Through other adoptees, I get to experience the emotional resolution that I was denied. Each successful case completes me.

MEANT TO BE

I never had the reunion of my childhood fantasies. My contact with Priscilla was an introduction to the dark side of the human heart, and it robbed me of the closure I'd yearned for my whole life. What I did get, however, was a career. As I continued to hunt relentlessly for my own blood relatives, I got pretty deft at the kind of research work it takes to negotiate through all those records. I was tenacious. Lydia's intuition and my own process of trial and error taught me how to ask the right questions, and to intuit what a particular set of circumstances could mean. The compassion and kindness of strangers gave me the lucky breaks I needed along the way.

I found my calling, and for that, I will be forever grateful. Even though I didn't have a happy reunion with my own birth mother, being able to give that to other adoptees has become my passion. I'm good at this—damn good. Because my own search was so difficult, there isn't a single road that my clients are going down that I haven't already walked myself. I know what they are thinking and feeling. I've been through the whole roller coaster of emotions, and I can guide them about what to expect, and how to prepare for what's next. This is *exactly* what I was meant to do.

The Lesson: Be Prepared

Don't assume that the person you are looking for is going to be the carbon copy of what you think and want. We, as adoptees, assume the people we are looking for, because they are genetically related, are going to be just like us. We have to take a step back and consider that the person we are looking for may not want to be found. We also have to realize that we may not like the person we find. Ultimately, you are who you are, regardless. Your genetics do not define you. So look, hope for the best, but make sure you are prepared for any outcome, good or bad.

I learned this the hard way. Not only was my birth mother not like me, I never even entertained the possibility that I could dislike her. When you search for someone your whole life, believing they will be just like you and they are not, it leaves you reeling. You wonder where you fit in.

Sadly, Priscilla has never been able to get past the pain of rejection in her own life. I had imagined that giving me up was one of the most painful experiences she had ever endured, and I'd hoped that I would be able to assure her that she had made the right decision and that I was okay and grateful. But emotionally, she was in a much different place. I was searching for the superpower version of Pam—a woman who would be everything I wanted to grow up to be. I was not searching for a replacement of my adoptive mother. I was really looking for a piece of myself, and what I learned is that strength and identity was partly DNA but mostly came from love and nurturing by my adoptive family.

Had I not plunged into the search headfirst, I would have had that perspective, and it might have cushioned the blow. So do your homework, educate yourself on the process, be prepared for any outcome, and make sure you have an excellent support system.

CHAPTER TWO

The Little Black Book

• • •

He was a straight-shooting Texan businessman with power, influence, and enough money to buy most of what he could ever need. He had the contacts and resources to hire the best private investigators. But each time he did, the result was the same: no luck. For all his millions, John Knox couldn't find his birth mother. For forty years, her identity had remained a mystery, and it was starting to look like she'd never be found. But John refused to accept defeat. She must have existed at some time, in some place. And he had to know.

It was the fall of 1997 and I was starting to build a real reputation for myself in the adoption search business. I'd already cracked my share of seemingly impossible cases and I was starting to feel like it was time for me to branch out on my own. One of the first adoption search agencies I worked with would lure in clients by raising their hopes, and charge them whether they found their birth parents or not. I couldn't be associated with that kind of business practice. These people were exploiting the desperation of people who were just like me.

I bounced between two more search agencies before I finally ended up at a large private detective agency in Long Island called Priority One. Again, it wasn't an ideal situation for me, but they kept me busy. I quickly became the go-to girl for all of the agency's adoption searches. If it was a cold case, they handed it to me, figuring they had nothing to lose. Once I got my teeth into it, I was like a dog with a bone. If I wasn't supposed to know, it would spur me on even more. A closed file was something I just couldn't accept. But the John Knox case was the toughest one I'd seen yet.

John had already gone through two agencies before he found Priority One. He lost count of how many hundreds of thousands of dollars he'd wasted on dead ends. It didn't help that he had been born in Colorado, a state with some of the tightest adoption secrecy laws in the country. Back in the day, unwed moms-to-be would travel there from all over the country for that very reason.

John's dossier was several inches thick. Over the years, the people he'd hired had gone through millions of names from hundreds of databases. They'd been searching in three states. Various clues came and went, but they led nowhere. The investigation was about to run out of steam. That's when I got the call. John made it clear I was his last best hope. "Well, Pam, I hear you're a miracle worker and I pray it's true," he said.

Born in Denver, Colorado, on February 21, 1955, and raised in Texas, he was brought home when he was just six weeks old. It was a loving and supportive family. They sent him to great schools and raised him with Christian values and a solid work ethic. His father was a successful entrepreneur and his mother had great business skills of her own. To this day, John credits the example of both parents with his ability to build one of the most successful surety and bond businesses in the country. He mentioned several times that he'd had a great childhood and loved his adoptive parents very much.

He'd always known he was adopted. Since he could remember, John was curious about his birth mother, but he assumed he would never find her. And if he ever did, he wasn't expecting the truth to be pretty.

"I'm not one of these people who sentimentalize their birth

parents," he told me. "In fact, I'm pretty sure my birth mother has some kind of hard-luck story. Either she was a teenager who'd been knocked up, or a prostitute. I am assuming she doesn't even know who the father is."

Too often, my clients harbor the fantasies that their birth mother was some nice young girl from a strict family who was forced to give up the baby because they couldn't have the scandal of a child born out of wedlock. They imagine her as an educated, virtuous woman who slipped up. Maybe she had an affair with a married man and she made the sacrifice to avoid breaking up the family. Who knows. Maybe the father was a Kennedy. I personally hoped my mother was Ivana Trump. It usually turns out to be a happy story. Most birth mothers really were good people undergoing difficult life circumstances. Sometimes fantasy lives up to reality. But part of my job is to manage expectations and prepare my clients for the absolute worst-case scenario.

I was glad John had prepared himself for a less than pretty story. He seemed unusually levelheaded. But I had to be sure. It was becoming clear his search had grown into an obsession that was taking over his life.

"So what are you hoping to get out of this, John? Why this burning desire to know?" I asked.

"It started out as a desire to know my biological history for medical reasons. I'm not getting any younger, and now I have three young children to worry about. But . . . there's a little more to it than that."

"Go on."

John let out a sigh that expressed years of reflection and self-questioning.

"I'm not really sure where this is coming from other than no matter how content you are with your life, that curiosity is always there, you know?"

I knew all right.

"You think you'll get used to it and learn to deal with not

knowing, but it catches up with you eventually. There's just some-thing about where you come from. You can't escape it. And now I've got the time, and I've got the money. I can't rest until I have my answers."

He filled me in on the journey so far. In his early twenties, he happened to be in Denver on business, and on an impulse he went to the local Bureau of Vital Statistics. His adoptive birth certificate had a long number with a "-B" at the end of it, and on a hunch he asked for the record with that same number, but with a "-A," and almost got away with it. But just as the clerk was about to make a copy of it, she stopped herself. "I'm sorry, sir. I can't give this to you without a court order. This file is sealed."

FORT KNOX

John talked to a lawyer, who told him the laws in Colorado were tough and that a court order was unlikely. So he left it at that. He was too busy building a life and a business to allow himself to get consumed by the search. For now, it was time to move on.

He settled down, got married, and had three sons. By 1994, as he was approaching forty, the searching bug bit him again. He'd just sold the first insurance company he'd founded for a king's ransom and now he had more time on his hands. His el-dest son, who was eight at the time, had just been diagnosed with an attention-deficit/hyperactivity disorder (ADHD). John needed to know if it ran in his birth family.

He went back to the Bureau of Vital Statistics in Colorado. Once again, the clerk could not be persuaded to give up the file, but she gave him a valuable tip: He could get a court order in Texas, which would be a hell of a lot easier than in Colorado. John didn't think they'd recognize a court order out of state, and that's usually the case. But this kindhearted bureaucrat said she'd recognize it. So John went back to Houston, hired a lawyer, and got a doctor's note explaining his son's medical condition and his need to see the original birth records. Within days, court order in hand, John was back in Denver. When he was handed this document, he was excited. Finally, this lifelong mystery would be solved.

The birth certificate named him as "Baby Boy Sinclair." The birth mother was listed as Barbara Sinclair. There was an address, but he didn't give it a second thought.

His next step was to go to the Catholic Charities office where he'd been adopted. The people there were willing to give him any non-identifying information about his birth mother. She was twenty-seven when she had him and she came from a large, well-to-do family from New Jersey. She had five other siblings, and her father was a prominent banker. The file gave the exact ages of the siblings as well as her date of birth, and stated that she was Catholic.

COLD TRAIL

John felt like he was finally getting close. He started an intensive search, looking for all the large Catholic families named Sinclair in New Jersey in which siblings had similar ages and profiles. He hired a private investigator and law firms in Dallas and Denver. He gave one of his top executives a two-month leave of absence to go to Newark and oversee the investigation. He scoured the public records in New Jersey and the New York Public Library. He spent thousands of man-hours trying to match up profiles. There was just one problem. When he went back to the Catholic Charities for more information, he was told that Sinclair was not his birth mother's real name. Of course, they could not disclose her true identity. John's guy in Newark told him it was probably hopeless.

"But I had no doubt in my mind. I was even more determined that we were going to find her," he told me.

FORGOTTEN DETAIL

The pressure was on. I could not disappoint this man. After studying his file for a few days, I had a feeling they'd been looking in the wrong places all along. I called him.

"Hi, John. I think there's one lead we haven't yet explored. Pipe down!"

"Excuse me?"

"Oh, sorry, not you, John. My kids. Quiet, Ronnie! Mommy's on the phone!"

At this point, I had screaming and yelling in stereo in the background. I had two boys—a toddler and a seven-year-old, and they were as mischievous as boys that age can be. I was worried John might be having second thoughts—I sounded more like a harried suburban mom than a professional genealogist. It just so happened I was both.

"Did you ever check out that address in Denver where your mother was staying?"

"I drove past it, but it was nothing more than a run-down old house."

"Well, that's where we should look first. The place where it all started. Give me a few days."

It didn't take long to trace the address in Denver. It was a home for unwed mothers that was one of the most prominent back in the fifties. Thousands of women had passed anonymously through its doors. The place had been shuttered years ago. The woman who had run it had dementia, so she wouldn't have been much help to me. But I did manage to track down her children. The daughter wasn't so helpful. But her brother, Bob, was very chatty and friendly. I kept him on the phone for at least an hour and learned a lot about the home, the girls who went there, and what his mother had done for them.

The home was part of a system cloaked in darkness. Colorado has only just begun to roll back some of the laws that have sealed adoption records for baby boomers for decades. Maternity homes were hideouts where women, mostly young and unmarried, could have their babies in total secrecy and be assured that when they surrendered them for adoption, the fact that they were ever there would be sealed in closed state files forever. These women had probably felt they had no choice. It was postwar America, before *Roe v. Wade*. This was the dark side of the baby boom. Getting pregnant outside of marriage was completely taboo. The shame ran so deep that for many of these mothers—often Catholic girls from nice families—it was either this or suicide. They told no one—not their family members, not their friends. Only the midwives and the people who ran these homes had any knowledge of what had happened. And they falsified the paper trail to make sure it stayed that way. The information I gathered from Bob gave me a lot of insight about what John's birth mother must have gone through. As soon as I got off the phone with him, I called John. It was as if he'd gotten one step closer to knowing the woman who gave him life.

"It says a lot about that time and the thought process of those girls," he said. "It must have been an incredibly lonely and difficult time for my birth mother."

DEEP THROAT

Bob was a treasure trove of information. We spoke regularly over the course of a few days. I could tell he had a heart. We became friends over the phone and talked about many things—faith, family, how he liked to go fishing on the Colorado River. He was flattered to be asked so many questions about his family's business. But I knew he wasn't being completely straight with me. In our last conversation, he told me they'd destroyed all the records of the women who'd stayed at the home. One of the only ways for adoptees to find the real names of their birth mothers was to sue, and Bob and his sister had been dragged through civil court more than thirty times. He said it had cost them so much money, they'd closed up shop and destroyed all the records. I wasn't buying it.

"Oh, come on, Bob, all of them, really?"

"Um, yes, as I recall. . . ."

"Well, okay, Bob, if you say so. I know you're a good Christian guy, and if you could help someone out, you would. You know that John has some medical issues, and it's vital for the sake of his health, and the health of his kids, that he find out a few things about his birth parents. If there was some way to help, I'm sure you'd step up."

"Aaaw, Pam, you're killing me! Okay, let me see what I can do."

I could tell he was feeling guilty. I left a voice-mail message for John and told him what I'd learned, and how helpful Bob might be to us. The next morning, I got a call.

"Hey, Pam, it's me, John. I'm at the airport. I'm gonna go meet Bob in person."

"Nooo! You can't! What if you say something that makes him suspicious? It could blow everything! Please don't get on that plane!"

"I'm going. Bye."

That was just like John. He's a success in business because he tackles a problem head-on and refuses to wait around and let someone else fix it. He just jumps on a plane and goes. But I was nervous. I had been purposely vague with Bob, and I couldn't remember everything I'd said to him on the phone. I hadn't lied about who I was, but I may have let him assume I was just a concerned sister or friend. I tend to play up my harried suburban mom persona in certain situations because it's less threatening. It makes people comfortable and gets them talking. Somehow, people sense the sincerity of my intentions. I am forthright about what I am trying to accomplish and, as a result, they trust me.

THE BREAKTHROUGH

John rented a car and drove to Bob's address. He found him sitting on his driveway in a lawn chair, enjoying a few beers in the afternoon sunshine. John struck up a conversation and told him outright who he was and how anxious he was to find his birth mother for medical reasons. He even showed Bob the doctor's letter about his son. Bob was sympathetic. John laid on all his Texas charm. But Bob continued to insist that all the records had been destroyed. He explained how strict the Colorado laws were about privacy, and how important it was to all the women who'd stayed at the home that no one ever find out about it. He even went into detail about how they'd falsified their records, mentioning a little black book they'd used as an entry log. John continued the conversation for another hour or so. Then it came to him in a flash.

"Bob, your sister has the black book, doesn't she?"

"No. I am sure that's been destroyed, too."

Up until that point, Bob had been making direct eye contact with John, but then he started looking down, around, and up—anywhere but straight at him. He was the world's worst liar. John persisted with his questions. He found out that Bob's mother would make log entries of all the girl's actual names and places of residence. In the next column, she would write down the fake name and state. The name was usually one letter off, and the state listed was usually adjacent to the actual state where the girl resided. So John had been searching in the wrong place all along. New Jersey was, in fact, New York.

Bob told John it was useless. His sister wouldn't talk to anyone. John left, and when he got back to Texas, he wrote to Bob, reiterating the fact that he wasn't an intermediary and he had no interest in litigating or making Bob's and his sister's lives difficult. He was just there for himself, and for the sake of his son. He gave Bob all his background information and pleaded for help. A week later, he got a call from Bob's sister, offering to help by making a few phone calls.

Two days later, early in the morning, Bob's sister called again.

"I'm so sorry. I wanted to help you, so I made some phone calls back where your birth mother used to live, and nobody knows where she is," she told John.

"Well, I really appreciate your trying," he replied.

John felt groggy. He was about to hang up the phone, when she said, "But do you want her name and old address anyway?"

"Hell yeah!"

As it turned out, John's birth mother used to live in Rockville Centre, Long Island. I had a name and a location. That was all I needed. By the end of the day, I'd found everything. Her details were an exact match to the non-identifying information. I'll call her Kathleen. She'd moved several times throughout her life, and now she was living in Sacramento, California. I phoned John with her unlisted address and number. His lifelong search was over. Mission accomplished!

CAUTIOUS APPROACH

John thought long and hard about how he would contact her. She'd probably kept his existence a secret his whole life, and the last thing he wanted was to cause her distress. Instead of a phone call, he decided to send her a letter by FedEx. But first he had his executive assistant call her and ask if she would be home the next day to sign for a package. He didn't want anyone else to get hold of it. He included the dossier with all the information he'd dug up during his long search for her. He also included information about himself, his family, and his company. And on top of this pile of information was a cover letter:

Dear Kathleen,

Two of the greatest things that have happened in my life are the fact that I was born, which some people take for granted, and the fact that I was adopted.

The note went on to describe his life, his search, and why it was so important for him to find her. He assured her he didn't want to upset her and that he would treat the matter with total confidentiality. But he felt strongly that it was his right to know her identity, if for no other reason than to learn his biological history and be better informed about any genetic health issues. He also asked if they could meet. He closed the letter with this:

The fall of 1954 and the spring of 1955 must have been very challenging for you. But please know that what must have been a difficult time in your life was the greatest thing that happened to me.

He tracked the FedEx package the next day. She signed for it, and two hours later, she called him.

"Hello, John. This is Kathleen. I just want you to know that I don't want to have any relationship. Nobody knows you exist. No one in my family. I don't want anyone to know about this."

John was unfazed. "I can appreciate that," he said. "I have no problem with that. I am not out searching for a family or a relationship. But I think I am entitled to information. I have a right to contact you and a right to know the medical background, and anything you can share with me about that."

"I don't disagree," she replied.

They talked for about forty minutes. They were starting to click. She confessed she was shocked that he'd been able to find her. He told her about the search, and how much he'd gone through to find her. Finally, he said, "I want to meet you."

"I know. You mentioned that in your letter. I need to think about it for a couple of weeks."

"Kathleen, I've known you for all of forty minutes now and I can tell that all you are going to do is worry about it. I'll come to Sacramento tomorrow. We'll have lunch."

"Okay."

FACE-TO-FACE

The encounter took place on November 10, 1997, a date John will never forget. They met in a seedy bar on the other side of town from where Kathleen lived. Over the course of two hours, she ordered three Bloody Marys. It was a liquid lunch. She told him how she'd been involved with a man for four years in Europe. It ended, so she moved back to New York and got a job as a buyer in a Manhattan department store. Then she met a guy named Bill Heins, John's father, at a party. She described the liaison as "a very short relationship," although just how short was never defined. When she discovered she was pregnant, at twenty-eight, she did her research and found out the one place she could have the baby where no one would ever find out. She had no choice. It was either that or total shame and ostracism from her tightly knit, very Catholic family. Her father was a pillar of the town where she was from. He was also high up in the Federal Reserve. A scandal was out of the question.

She told her parents she had to travel for work, and she was assigned to another branch of the department store chain, clear across the country. She didn't go home for her sister's wedding. She was eight months pregnant at the time. She told her family that she was sick, but they never believed her. The suspected lie caused a permanent rift between Kathleen and her sister, with whom she had been especially close. Things were never quite the same with her family thereafter.

She never saw John after he was born. Almost immediately, she moved back to New York. A year later, she was married. Soon after, she started having more children—five in total. She told John she'd never looked back: "I never had a moment's regret about putting you up for adoption. It was the right thing to do."

But later in the conversation, she admitted something. Every February, without fail, she'd fall into a depression so severe she could not even get out of bed. It usually started a few days before John's birthday, and continued for weeks. This went on for years. And while she was grieving over the loss of her firstborn, she left her very confused and concerned husband to look after their brood of young children. It got so bad, she even went to a psychiatrist, which was considered an extreme step in those days. Apart from the staff of the maternity home, her shrink was the only other person who ever knew about John.

Over the course of the afternoon, John and Kathleen really hit it off.

"I like you, John," she said. "I mean, I really, really like you. One day after I'm gone, you should look up my kids. You'd get along great."

John thought it would be a bit strange to look up his half siblings and tell them their mother had been lying to them all those years. But he understood her motive. She was protecting her husband, who was still alive. She had put him through hell, and she knew how hurt he'd be if he found out she'd been keeping that secret from him all this time. The driving force of her desire for anonymity was love.

At one point, John asked her about his father.

"You don't need to bother looking him up. That sorry son of a bitch!" she said.

But she gave John everything he wanted: the full medical history of the family, pictures of herself when she was younger, snapshots of his siblings. It turns out that ADHD did run in her side of the family. But, thankfully, cancer and heart disease did not. Whatever he asked for in terms of information from Kathleen, he got, and more. In exchange, he respected her need for confidentiality. He never intruded on her life again. As much as he wanted to see her once more, he never called or wrote. He left that up to her.

As he walked Kathleen to her car, she told him that she'd love to meet his wife and children one day. "Maybe we can all get together at your house in Texas and have a barbecue. I'll bring some Californian wine," she said.

Instinctively, John knew it would never happen. The last he heard from her was a "Thinking of You" card postmarked from Hawaii. That was ten years ago.

THE PLAYBOY

While all this was going on, I was busy hunting for John's birth father. It was a heck of a lot easier than finding his birth mom. I tracked down Bill Heins through his children. Bill's son, Billy, worked on Wall Street and had built a name for himself in the bond trade. I told him I was doing genealogy research on the Heins family in New York. He was only too happy to fill me in on the family story.

Bill senior lived in Baldwin, New York, practically down the street from where Kathleen used to live in Rockville Centre. He got married in 1954, right after his relationship with John's mother. His first son from that marriage, Billy, was just seven months younger than John. Bill's other son, Jimmy, was born two years later. Their mother, Bill's ex-wife, had recently passed away. The family had lived a comfortable middle-class existence on Bill senior's salary as land commissioner for Nassau County. Bill had since retired and was running a small import business out of his home in Baldwin.

I called John and gave him the address. He happened to be in New York at the time, and had decided to drive out to Rockville Centre to check out his birth mother's family house. As he was nearby, he figured he'd drop in on his dad in Baldwin, but he couldn't find the house. I phoned Bill senior to make sure he was home and told him my research assistant was stopping by to drop off the completed genealogy research report. I think old Bill was starting to suspect we were process servers by now. When John showed up, Bill sat him down in his office and started talking nonstop. He went on for a while. Finally, John said, "Bill, do you mind if I talk for just a minute?"

"Sure!"

"I was born on February 21, 1955."

"Oh."

"My birth mother is from Rockville Centre, New York."

"Well, that's just down the street."

"Yeah, that's what I understand."

Bill looked over his shoulder and then at John. "Do you think you're my son?" he asked.

"That's kind of where this is going."

Bill was overjoyed. At first, he couldn't remember John's birth mother (there'd been a number of women back in the day), but he was thrilled and proud of the fact that he'd fathered a son, especially a fine and upstanding man like John. John quickly realized he'd given Kathleen's married name, so he reminded his birth father about her again. Bill senior looked sheepish. "Oh yeah, her," he said.

The pair started to catch each other up on their lives, but Bill was emotional. He had tears in his eyes. He kept getting up to give John a hug.

"Oh my God, I can't believe I have another son!"

Bill wanted to know all about John's family and kids. He kept asking him to come back for another visit and meet his two half brothers. That night, when John got back to his hotel room, the phone was ringing. It was Jimmy, the younger brother. "Billy and I have to meet you. Can we come over?" he asked John.

BROTHERLY LOVE

They arrived at the hotel the next morning for breakfast, and the long-lost brothers connected right away. They talked and laughed for half the morning, telling John how nervous they'd been getting about all of my inquisitive phone calls. Billy's wife had told him she was sure it was about an illegitimate child, either Billy's or Bill's.

John particularly hit it off with Jimmy. They were kindred spirits. Today, they talk on the phone at least twice a week. They're brothers in the truest sense.

On another trip, John was sitting next to his birth father at dinner in the Rainbow Room in Manhattan when Billy and Jimmy burst out laughing. They were struck by how similar father and son were. John and Bill senior had identical mannerisms and facial expressions. Without either of them realizing it, when Bill rested his chin in his hand, so did John. When the father raised an eyebrow, so did John. They even had the same laugh. Genetics are a powerful thing.

That year, Bill senior sent Christmas presents to John's kids in Texas. The following year, he went down to visit them. And there have been numerous visits back and forth between the families ever since.

This was far more than John had expected to gain from his search. His existence was fully embraced by his proud birth father. And as complicated and sad as his birth mother's situation was, he had no doubt that the bond he and his father had was very real.

"It's like completing a puzzle. All the pieces fit. There are some core, fundamental things about me that I never knew until I found my birth parents," John said.

There was just one sour note. My employer, Priority One, charged John close to ten thousand dollars for its services, more than three times the usual client fee, and many, many times more than my cut. I was disgusted. The agency knew he had the money and that he was desperate. I quit, then called John to let him know what happened and how sorry I was. I didn't want him to think I'd had any part in it.

John got what he wanted, and he gave me the confidence to strike out on my own. It wouldn't be easy, but cracking that next-to-impossible case told me I had what it would take to build my own business—the kind of business that would treat people like John with all the respect and compassion they deserved.

The Lesson: Never Give Up

Persistence is key. If a search is important enough to someone, that person has to keep going, no matter how many obstacles stand in the way. It's common for my clients to pick up the search and put it down again. The psychology is that if they have exhausted all their efforts, their hope evaporates. In their minds, leaving stones unturned keeps the hope alive. They can always feel like there is more they can do.

But John Knox never gave up. He tried everything he knew how to do. He threw all of his considerable resources at it, until eventually something worked. Even though some birth records are falsified, there is almost always an element of truth within the information at hand. It's my job as a searcher to figure out what that truth is. In John's case, the address on his birth certificate was key. That's what led me to locate the maternity shelter and the family who had the records. That's what broke a seemingly impossible case. But what really made it happen was the fact that John never lost hope.

CHAPTER THREE

A Line in the Steam

◆ ◆ ◆

I believe most adoptees have that moment of realization. Whether it happens early, when as a toddler you can first comprehend, or later in life; whether you always sort of knew, subconsciously, or you found out by accident when going through your parents' papers; whether your adoptive parents gently told you how they "picked" you, and that is why you are loved so much—from that moment on, your worldview will shift. Nothing will ever be as it once seemed.

For Sheila Jaffe, that moment came on a street corner in the Bronx. She was eleven years old, and she was in the middle of a fight with a neighborhood girl, Myrna, when the kid blurted out, "Your parents don't care about you anyway. No one wants you. You're adopted!"

Of course, this rocked Sheila's world. Back in those days, the 1960s, being adopted was not something that was spoken about openly. It was a stigma. At first, Sheila didn't believe what Myrna had said. It was just another nasty taunt—something prepubescent girls whispered to their friends to cast you as "different." But Sheila couldn't let it go. There was something about the way her friends reacted when the neighborhood bully broadcast this supposed slur to the entire street. "Okay, gotta go do my homework now. Uh, see ya!" one of them said before they all scattered to the four winds.

Being the ballsy type, Sheila confronted her parents the instant she got home. When they refused to address the issue, she called her best friend, Karen, who lived two floors up from Sheila in the same apartment building. Sheila asked her to come over right away. She wanted to see the look on her friend's face.

"Karen, Myrna said I was adopted today. I know it's true and you know it, too!" Sheila said to Karen.

When Sheila said this to Karen, she had no idea if it was true or not—she was just testing the waters—but that one look gave her the answer. Karen's face got beet red and she started to cry. The girls had never had any secrets between them before, but the whole neighborhood knew Sheila had been adopted. Sheila's mother wasn't pregnant, and one day she came home with a baby, so it was pretty obvious.

"Sheila, I'm so sorry! My mother told me to never tell!"

Sheila's parents stood by in the living room, obviously frightened. As Karen left, Sheila's father looked catatonic. Sheila overheard her mother's urgent whisper to him: "We have to tell her; we have to tell her."

This comment was just added confirmation of what Sheila now knew for a fact, but she still needed her parents to acknowledge it to her face. They couldn't. Like so many adoptive parents in those days, they feared that if they admitted to the adoption, their child would want to be with her "real family." Her father's fear of losing his little girl, who was his world, paralyzed him. What Sheila didn't know at the time, and only found out years later through relatives, was that they'd almost lost her once before, when she was still a baby. There's a probation period in some adoptions, and the handover of the child isn't complete until the birth mother signs a form, thereby releasing her child to the adoptive family. But Sheila's birth mother had disappeared before that could happen. Without the signed documents, Sheila's adoptive parents had to go to court to fight for custody, or risk losing Sheila to the foster-care system. Her father still hadn't gotten over the trauma.

"He loved me and I loved him, but he shut down because he was just not emotionally equipped to deal with this," Sheila said later.

Her mom took over. She announced to Sheila that they would all be going to the doctor the next day. "Daddy's going to come home early and he's going to meet us there," she said.

Sheila did not have the words to say, *Just tell me.* Instead, she rebelled. "No, I'm not sick! I don't want to go to the doctor!"

"We're going!" her mother replied.

It was the best way her parents knew to deal with the situation, but the doctor's office was a cold and clinical place to deliver a message like that. Sheila remembers thin walls with a small shuttered partition between the waiting room and the doctor's office. You could hear everything through those walls. Sheila was summoned in to see the doctor while her anxious mother and father waited outside. She was directed to a chair opposite the doctor's desk and told to sit down.

"Everything felt oversized in that room. I was this little peanut sitting in a big leather chair that was swallowing me up, with a big doctor behind a big mahogany desk. I felt like Alice in Wonderland," Sheila recalled.

The doctor told her that her parents loved her very much. Sheila could hear her parents through the door. They were saying, "Yes, we do!" He then proceeded to give Sheila a cock-and-bull story about her birth parents—two people who were very much in love, but young and in college, and unable to afford to keep her. This was why her parents had taken her home.

"Sheila, do you understand?" the doctor asked.

She nodded.

"Do you have any questions?"

"*No*," she replied.

Sheila received all this information like a good little girl. She felt like a patient receiving the diagnosis of what was wrong with her. She was in shock, but she was too young to articulate these complex emotions. She ran out of the office and into her mother's arms, bawling her eyes out. When she stopped crying and wiped her tears, she looked up at her mother and asked, "Who is she? Who is my mother?"

Then her mother said a very unfortunate thing: "Oh, any cat can have kittens."

"Don't you call my mother a cat!" Sheila cried.

Her mother was just scared and defensive. She didn't mean it. But Sheila was stung. She hated her mother for years afterward. Her father was no use in the situation. He was speechless.

REBELLIOUS YOUTH

Looking back, Sheila realized she'd had a sense she was adopted from the time she first understood the concept, and long before the fact was confirmed. But she worshipped her father, and every time the thought bubbled up from the back of her mind that they might not be related by blood, she shoved it aside. Her adoption revelation set the tone for the rest of her developing years. It turned her into a rebel. Think of her as a Jewish version of Rizzo in the movie *Grease*. She was a little hottie with dark hair, olive skin, and sky-high cheekbones, always looking for trouble. Sheila was one of the smartest girls in school, but between the ages of eleven and fourteen, she chose to hang out with the stupidest kids in the Bronx. She left all her old friends—the ones who had hidden the truth from her—and went to the other side. She also sought out foster kids and gang members to be her friends, because they seemed just as lost as she was.

"I felt like I was the bad girl who got given away. Who cared anyhow?" she explained later.

Every so often, she'd be reminded that she was different, like the time she was asked to draw a family tree in middle school, or during a health class in high school when the teacher started talking about the fact that male-pattern baldness comes from the mother's side of the family. These were random pieces of information she didn't have, and it bothered her.

"Somehow, it really pissed me off that I would never know if my maternal grandfather was bald," Sheila said.

Sheila felt increasingly isolated. She didn't know any other kids who were adopted, so she had no one to relate to. It forced her to carve out her own path. Because Sheila was so bright and driven, she would eventually turn that restless energy into becoming one of Hollywood's biggest power players. Today, she's the casting director for all the hottest movies and television shows, from *Rambo* to *Entourage* and *The Sopranos*.

When Sheila was fourteen, she decided to take the first steps on her search. Without explaining why, she asked her parents for the name of the hospital in Manhattan where she was born. She was mature-looking for her age, so she got dressed up and asked a friend to go into town with her. Sheila marched into what was then known as Manhattan General Hospital and gave the particulars of her name and birth date. She explained she was adopted and wanted to know who her birth mother was. The receptionist almost exploded with laughter. Unable to wipe the smirk off her face, she explained to the child that there was no way she could ever divulge that information. Sheila's birth records were sealed.

Sheila was deflated. She'd just assumed it was her right to know. It never occurred to her that there would be all this secrecy, and that, as far as the state was concerned, she could never have the answers she craved. But she never gave up. She didn't look like the rest of her adoptive family, who were blond and blue-eyed. So when she'd see someone in the street or in a magazine who looked even remotely like her, exotic, with dark hair and dark eyes, she'd wonder if that person was related to her.

"People tell you someone looks like she could be your sister and your head goes off in all these different directions," she explained.

Like most adoptees, she was stealthy in her efforts to find her birth family. She was desperate for that piece of her history—the first chapter, which most people take for granted. When she told people she was adopted, their reactions were almost always the same: "Oh my God, I am so sorry!" or "Do you know who your real parents are?"

The assumptions and ignorance she encountered stuck in her side like thorns. But she didn't want to hurt her parents, especially her dad. She was glad she was raised a Jaffe and she loved both her parents. They were older, as many adoptive parents are, and they'd fought hard to have Sheila in their lives. Her mother was a housewife and her father made patterns at a garment factory—Jaffe Pleating—that was owned by his brother. They were comfortably middle-class, but they didn't have much money, so Sheila's uncle helped pay for the private adoption, which almost didn't go through. When Sheila had turned thirty, her mother and father died within a year of each other, and she always regretted any pain or insecurity she may have caused them.

"I just wanted to shout, 'You are my parents! You are the ones I love!' But it was too late."

Over the years, she kept dabbling in the search for her birth parents. The desire to know never left her, but there weren't many resources available when she was younger. Such a search takes determination and courage. It's a brave thing to look for your birth family when you don't know what you are going to find, or how you are going to find it. But then, Sheila's a very gutsy woman. Her first move was to obtain her birth family's non-identifying information. It said that her birth mother was a twenty-six-year-old schoolteacher and her father was a restaurant proprietor. It revealed little else, which of course was the intention, but the blanked-out names and veil of secrecy infuriated her.

"That document was the stupidest thing I ever read," she recalled.

She eventually joined Adoptees' Liberty Movement Association (ALMA), a society dedicated to adoptee reunion and the reform of adoption laws. ALMA supports adoptees' in their searches and publishes booklets with tips. It tells you how to go to the public library to find the name you were born under by matching up birth dates and birth certificate numbers. Sheila learned that her birth name was Shack (she was listed only as "Female Shack" in the book of birth records). She reached out to every Shack family in the tristate area and wrote to all of them.

"I did all of the things that you would think to do," she said.

SLEEPING WITH STRANGERS

When Marty Shack wrote back to her from Long Island, thinking he might be her brother, Sheila paid his family a visit. But when she stepped through their door, the statuesque brunette thought she'd arrived in Munchkinland. Every single one of the Shack siblings was short and blond. It was patently obvious there was no relation. Just to be polite, Sheila stayed for a while and flipped through some family albums, but nothing clicked. Adding to her embarrassment, she missed the last train back to Manhattan and had to spend the night with these strangers.

There were no other nibbles. It had been a private adoption, and those are the toughest to crack. It wasn't long before Sheila hit a wall. Without an agency acting as intermediary in an adoption, there is less of a paper trail. Through the extensive network of adoptees she'd built up over the years, Sheila finally came into contact with my old friend Lydia. Lydia did a search and located a family in Berkeley, California. Or I should say, I located the family. I wasn't involved in the whole case, but at the end of the search, Lydia asked me to track down the address for her.

Lydia did everything right. She followed every lead, and, on paper at least, it appeared this had to be the right family, down to the fact that the birth mother had been living in New Mexico as a teacher around the time Sheila was conceived. But Lydia warned Sheila that there was always a possibility she might be wrong. All the pieces can seem to fit, but you have to meet someone face-to-face and go with your gut. From what I'd heard, I didn't feel good about this situation. It was clear the family Lydia had found wanted nothing to do with Sheila, at least not initially. I didn't really know Sheila at this point—I was just helping Lydia finish a particularly tough job—but I called Sheila to give her a heads-up. I said, "I just want you to know that I've been speaking to the woman Lydia identified as your birth sister, and this lady is tough. I don't want you to be disappointed when you meet her."

Nothing would stop her now, however. Sheila divides her time between L.A. and New York, so she tried to arrange a meeting with her birth family when she next had to be on the West Coast. She wrote to the alleged sister, who at first insisted the relationship wasn't possible. They spoke a few more times. Sheila kept the door open and stayed in touch. Finally, the woman agreed to a meeting.

Sheila flew up from Los Angeles to San Francisco, rented a car, and drove into Berkeley, where she booked herself into a hotel. She arranged to meet this woman at a nearby restaurant. When she walked in, she looked nothing like Sheila.

"She was not the most attractive person in the world," Sheila remarked later.

Something about this lady seemed off, as if she was mildly autistic. There was no sustained eye contact, and it was a struggle for her to connect with Sheila on any level. Evidently, the woman had had a hard life. But she was trying, and so was Sheila. She had brought pictures of her mother, but again, this woman looked nothing like Sheila. The woman mentioned a sister, now dead, who had been a paranoid schizophrenic. Sheila looked nothing like her, either. One cousin did look very much like Sheila, however, and it was enough to convince her that they were related. There was also a brother, but he wanted nothing to do with this. Sheila never saw his picture.

MAYBE THIS TIME

Sheila and the strange woman from Berkeley took a DNA test together, and it came back as a low possibility they were related. Their curiosity was piqued and they both jumped on the potential connection. They'd warmed to each other by the end of an otherwise awkward dinner, and the woman invited Sheila for breakfast the next morning. She planned to introduce Sheila to the man she figured was probably Sheila's father—the love of her mother's life and the man she'd been seeing right around the time Sheila was born. He was of Swedish origin.

That night, Sheila's nerves were raw. She kept staring into the mirror and saying to herself, *I'm Swedish*. Her back felt like it was on fire and she couldn't sleep. The guy she'd been dating called to see how it was going and if she was okay. "I am all right," she told him.

"No, you're not. You sound terrible. Get on the next plane and come home. You don't need to do this."

"I can't go back now. I have to meet my father," she said.

Sheila spent part of the day at the house where her sister had spent most of her life with her mother. It felt strange. In the afternoon, the two women headed off to Oakland, where the alleged dad lived. His name was Howard, and he was a sweetheart. He'd invented something and had become very wealthy. He had a wife and family and lived a good life. They arranged to take a DNA test, but it turned out that he was not a match, although he wished he was.

"Why do you say that, Howard?" Sheila asked.

"So you could put your mind at ease," he told her.

Sheila had a lot of questions about her mother. Howard said Sheila was nothing like her. He wasn't very complimentary about his old flame. He stopped just short of calling her a shameless tramp. "Let's just say I was a merchant marine and I always knew when I was away there was someone else in bed with her. She just liked to fool around."

Sheila kept in touch with the woman from Berkeley. She even slept over at her house on a later visit. For two years, that was her other family. But something was nagging away at the back of her mind. She felt like she was flirting with another family and that she was cheating on the Jaffes. These people she'd discovered were nothing like the people who had raised her and taken care of her when she had the chicken pox. Everything felt a little forced.

A SENSE OF MISSION

By now, Sheila was deeply involved in adoptee support groups. She became close friends with Darryl McDaniels of Run—DMC, another adoptee who was equally passionate about opening up adoption records. The pair formed an organization called Felix to send foster children to camp and provide whatever support it could to let these kids know they were not alone. Sheila has developed special relationships with many of these kids over the years. She takes one little girl in particular on shopping sprees for summer clothes. When Sheila bought her a birthday present one time, the girl told her no one had ever bought her a gift before. She'd spent her life shunted from one foster home to the next—sixteen in all. It made Sheila realize how much she has to be thankful for, and how important it is for her to give back.

"At the end of the day I am just me. My birth mother had the seed that put me here, and I was adopted so that one day I could do something for these kids. It was my destiny," she explained.

Sheila has a godson who is adopted, and she adores the kid. When she asked him how he felt about where he came from, he said he literally thinks of himself as having been dropped from the sky. Sheila loves to quote him: "My birth mother couldn't catch me, so my real mother did."

There's a sense of identity you get from being adopted—a worldview that's unique. When you bond with other adoptees in support groups, they become like a tight-knit family of misfits. You feel protective of one another. Sheila and Darryl understand each other on a level no one else could. They both know it could so easily have gone the other way for them. They could have ended up as orphans, with no stable home life and none of the advantages that have made them the incredibly successful human beings they are today.

When Darryl decided to make a documentary about his adoption journey, Sheila was the one who encouraged him to go forward with this project to help inspire other adoptees. When I met Darryl, I asked him how Sheila was doing, and his answer made me think something wasn't right. He gave me her number, and I reached out to her the next day.

"Sheila, this is Pam Slaton. You can say no if you want to, but I've been told that you're still searching, and I want to understand what's happening. Maybe I should take another look at your case."

"Be my guest! I'd love to get some more answers," she replied.

"Since I wasn't involved in the case from the beginning, please send me all the files you have, and I'll get to work."

Doubts about her most recent reunion with the woman from Berkeley had been haunting Sheila for a while, so she was only too happy to let me take a crack at the case. It took me a few weeks. Lydia had been handed a tough case and she'd done well with what she had, but by the time I was able to take another look, many online resources had become available to me. Lydia started her search with a family on Long Island and that took her to California. She got the trajectory right, but it was a different family. Sheila's birth mother's name was Clarice. Clarice was also a schoolteacher in New Mexico. We don't know a lot about the birth father, except that he might have been Mexican or Native American. Sheila thinks that would explain her high cheekbones and vaguely exotic features. Clarice was a nice Jewish girl in her twenties who'd slipped up, and she did what so many birth mothers of that era did: She went home to New York and gave Sheila up for adoption. Shortly after, perhaps to escape from the sad memories, Clarice moved to the West Coast and settled in Newport Beach. She married and had a son. But when I dug deeper, my heart sank. Clarice had passed away nine months earlier. She was in her eighties at the time, and she'd been sickly for quite a while. I just hate it when I'm too late.

BITTERSWEET

Sheila was in Los Angeles when I found out the truth. This was not the kind of news I wanted to pass along to her over the phone. I knew that Darryl was there at the time, so I reached out to him and asked him to take her to dinner and break it to her gently. At least that way, she could hear it from a close friend. Darryl told her in his own sweet, loving way. Sheila was crushed, but Darryl said, "Hey, look at it this way. Now you have a brother."

That night, Sheila called me. I felt horrible. But she didn't.

"I love you!" she said. "I want to marry you! You don't know what you just did for me."

It was as if the weight of the world had been lifted from her shoulders. She'd suppressed her doubts for so long, but now that her instincts were confirmed and she had all the right answers, she could move forward. She reunited with her brother, and it was all that it should be: uncomplicated and emotionally gratifying. She met all her cousins, aunts and uncles, and Leo, the man Clarice had married. He's ninety-seven but still very spry.

"He's kinda cool," said Sheila.

Leo knew about Sheila all along. He encouraged his wife to reach out to her, and he couldn't understand why she never did. I put it down to the usual reasons—shame and guilt. For birth mothers, these memories are too painful, so they get repressed. Leo told Sheila he knew his wife had suffered a lot from the loss of giving her up. Oddly, Clarice was a big follower of Hollywood news. She read the trades, even though she wasn't in the business, and the odds are she'd heard of Sheila. Whether she made the association that it was her daughter is unknown, but Sheila likes to think that her birth mother secretly knew, and that she was proud of her.

All this time, her birth family had been in her own backyard. She's since been to several family reunions and everyone in her extended family is thrilled to call her one of their own. But Sheila still has mixed feelings. Her first "reunion" prepared her for the roller-coaster ride of emotions and the feelings of guilt. But she still feels like she's cheating on her adoptive family. At a recent family reunion for one of the Jewish holidays, thirty family members and friends went around the table asking how everyone was related. "I got really pissy. I said I was

Sam and Helen's daughter, and no one knew who I was talking about," recalled Sheila, referring to the parents who raised her.

Sheila also feels some residual anger and resentment toward her birth mother. She wishes Clarice could have at least written her a letter saying who she was, where she was from, the reasons for giving her up, and the family's medical history. That alone might have been enough. Sheila recently went to the cemetery where Clarice had been cremated and saw her name on the wall. She spoke to the engraving: "Thanks for giving birth to me."

It was a kind of closure. But as always with these reunions, the emotions take some time to sort through. As much as Sheila enjoys knowing her birth family, she still hasn't quite figured out where they fit. They're not so different. It's a Jewish middle-class family of schoolteachers and professionals. One cousin is actually a film director. Some family members are musicians. Everyone gets along, although at times Sheila feels they are a little too friendly, perhaps because of who she is in the entertainment business.

"You wonder sometimes. Where do you put them? Do they even belong on your Christmas list?"

Sheila even felt conflicted when she received a picture of Clarice. She has a home in New York as well as in L.A., but somehow it seemed disloyal to put the photograph on the mantel in the city where her adoptive parents raised her. She knew she needed a frame for the photo in her Malibu apartment, because the salty sea air would damage it, but it took her months to decide which one to buy. The frame couldn't possibly be nicer than the ones used for the pictures of her adoptive family, so after about a month of deciding, she settled on something simple in Plexiglas. "I was so confused. I just didn't want Clarice to outshine my parents," she said.

Sheila's dilemma is one most of us face as adoptees. The

night she found out the real name of her birth mother, she was so excited. She finally had that missing piece of her identity. But then what? She took a shower and drew a line in the steam down the middle of the glass door on the shower stall. One side represented the Shack family, and the other side represented the Jaffe family. She didn't know which way to go. But she didn't have to choose. She was both.

The Lesson: Trust Your Gut

All the pieces of Sheila's search seemed to fit. It made sense on paper that the first person who was found was the biological mother. However, Sheila's inner voice said otherwise. If it feels wrong, it probably is. There is nothing like a face-to-face meeting to confirm or refute the findings of a search—DNA is generally conclusive, but that's not a perfect science, either. It is my own intuition that helps me solve my cases.

But also know that whatever you do find does not have to define you. Where do our alliances lie? You shouldn't even have to answer that question. As adoptees, we are made to feel that searching for our birth family is an indication of a want for more. It's taken to mean that we feel our adoptive families are not enough. It creates a feeling of disloyalty that shouldn't exist.

Knowing the birth family is important to our understanding of where we came from, but it doesn't necessarily mean we are trying to replace what we have or compensate for something that is missing. The fact is that we possess the capacity to love more than one family and we shouldn't be penalized for trying. A mother can love more than one child, so why shouldn't it be the other way around? Love should be limitless.

I am always amazed when people are challenged by anybody for wanting to search. Why not? We have a right to know the answer to that fundamental question: "Where do I come from?"

CHAPTER FOUR

The Rapper and the Housewife

◆ ◆ ◆

So what could a platinum-selling hip-hop legend and a housewife from New Jersey possibly have in common? You'd be surprised.

I first met Darryl "DMC" McDaniels in 2005, when he was working on a documentary for VH1 called *My Adoption Journey*, about his search for his birth mother. Of course, I was aware of his group, Run–DMC. Darryl and I were born two months apart, and you'd have to be living in a cave not to have heard "Walk This Way!"—his monster hit record with Aerosmith. I was a typical Italian-American girl from Queens who loved her eighties rock, and Run–DMC was the group that put rap on the radar for me and millions of other white suburban kids.

When I got the heads-up that Darryl would be contacting me, I was nervous. It would be my first experience doing my job on-camera, and with a celebrity no less. Even though I'd been at this for eleven years, this would be my first high-profile case, and the pressure was on. Ever since my disastrous contact with my own birth mother, I wasn't the outgoing girl I used to be. I had a level of social anxiety and I guess you could say I'd withdrawn from the outside world. I was more comfortable doing my job in the privacy of my little upstairs office, talking on the phone and hiding behind the computer. This new case was going to thrust me into the public eye and force me out of my shell. Ultimately, it would prove to be a good thing, but in the meantime the mere thought of this meeting gave me palpitations.

I was recommended to Darryl by Wendy Freund, a social worker at the New York Foundling Hospital. As one who operates inside the adoption system, she keeps a professional distance. But she'd referred a few cases to me in the past and she could see that Darryl's situation was right up my alley. This was one I could crack quickly. Darryl was privately adopted, but he went to the Foundling Hospital because it's the oldest agency in New York and he wanted advice on how to begin his search. He couldn't have chosen a better guide than Wendy. She is passionate about supporting birth families and adoptees on every level. But as much as she wants to help these people, she is bound by New York State laws not to give out any more than the non-identifying information in the file. She goes by the book, but when she can see adoptees are hitting a dead end, she gives them my number. With the documentary crew's cameras rolling, Wendy told Darryl I was "thorough and professional," and that I'd been adopted, too. Within minutes, Darryl was in his car and on his way to my house.

With what little information I had, I did a quick run-through my database. I couldn't find much. Then he called me from the road. "Hey, Pam, this is Darryl. I'm coming to see you!"

"Darryl! I'm looking forward to meeting you. I'm just trying to put together some information now."

"I believe in you, Pam. I know you can do this."

He was surprisingly soft-spoken and sweet. Immediately, I felt protective of him. I could hear in his voice how eager and scared he was. I could certainly relate. Your heart leaps into your throat every time you get a little scrap of information. But I was worried for him. The details were sketchy, and something about the name his adoptive parents gave him for his birth mother didn't add up.

To steady my nerves before Darryl's arrival, I took a swig of wine a few hours earlier in the day than I probably should have. I was overwhelmed by the fact that all of these cameras, and an entourage of producers and managers, were about to invade my home. When I saw the procession of cars pull up into my driveway half an hour after our phone conversation, I was shaking. I had to hold myself steady by gripping the end of my kitchen table.

But I had nothing to worry about. As soon as I opened my door, Darryl gave me a huge bear hug. Within minutes, I was in love. He was so open and vulnerable and had big, wide puppy dog eyes. He was incredibly kind and gracious to my family. There was none of that swagger you might expect from a hip-hop icon. He was a gentle soul, ready to connect with someone who'd been adopted herself. Darryl had felt alone on his quest for so long, and he needed a place where he could feel safe and understood.

TWO KIDS FROM QUEENS

As we talked, I discovered some weird parallels in our lives. Like me, Darryl had grown up in a middle-class family in Queens. He came from Hollis, which is about twenty minutes from my old neighborhood in College Point. Like mine, his adoptive parents were loving and hardworking, and they did everything they could to provide him with stability and a good education. Both Darryl and I went to parochial school. Like me, Darryl loved language, and he would express himself through poetry and rhymes (except that he turned his rhyming skills into a spectacular career). Like me, he'd always felt a little different from the rest of his family, despite the unconditional love and support they gave him. As was the case with me, his father, whom he adored, passed away shortly before he started his search. We appeared to be worlds apart on the surface, but our shared adoptee experience made for an intense bond. From the start, I knew what he was thinking and feeling. From the moment he showed up on my doorstep, I knew exactly where he was at on his emotional journey, because I'd been there, too.

The big difference between us was that Darryl's parents never admitted he was adopted until he was thirty-five years old. He discovered the truth when he was researching his autobiography. He asked his parents for more details about the day of his birth, because it occurred to him that the only thing he knew was the date. That's when they blurted out the truth. And they dropped this bombshell over the phone: "Son, we have something to tell you. You're adopted!"

"For real? Are you kidding me?"

"No. Your birth mother was sixteen years old, from the Dominican Republic. She was too young to raise you, so she gave you up for adoption."

"Well, who was she?"

"Bernada Lovelace. That's all we know. There's no information about your birth father. That's it."

At that moment, his whole life flashed backward. He was in shock.

Some members of the older generation prefer to keep adoption a secret. For them, it's a source of shame—something meant to be kept hidden forever. Parents think they are protecting their child, but denying the truth can actually be harmful, because when you don't know, you suspect; you grow up questioning everything about your existence. That's what Darryl was going through.

He'd always had a nagging suspicion, but Darryl buried this in the back of his mind. Neighborhood kids used to tease him because he looked nothing like his parents. "My father looked like Bill Cosby and my mom looked like Claire Huxtable," he said. "So I guess there wasn't much of a family resemblance."

Everybody suspected. "The mailman knew; all of my cousins knew. It was amazing how they were all able to keep a secret like that. Even the kids!"

When Darryl finally found out that he was adopted, his older cousin Donny told him he remembered being at his house the day he was brought home from the orphanage. Donny was four at the time, and his mother, Darryl's aunt, was asked to baby-sit while Darryl's mother ran out to the store to buy baby clothes. Darryl had nothing but the pair of cloth diapers he came in.

Donny's mother told him, "Under no circumstances are you to tell that effing McDaniels child he's adopted, you hear me?"

Darryl's home was where all the relatives and neighborhoods converged for Fourth of July cookouts and holiday dinners, yet no one told. All the kids feared a serious "ass whooping" if they blabbed. They were sat down and briefed by their parents every time they headed out for Darryl's house.

Darryl understands why they kept it a secret. He was a good kid who was doing well in school and they didn't want to risk upsetting him. They wanted everything about his life to seem as "normal" as possible. The fear was that if they told him, it would somehow ruin his whole existence. But all these years later, the lies and deception still hurt. Donny and Darryl were close. Donny practically grew up at Darryl's house.

"Yeah, I'm kinda angry that they created all these lies and second birth certificates, but I guess they figured, Don't rock the boat, because it's sailing just fine."

Looking back, there were a few clues. When Darryl first came to the McDaniels's home, he was a foster child, and he wasn't officially adopted until five years later. "I was a ward of the state, but I had no idea!" he said.

Darryl had wondered why his official birth certificate said 1969, when, in fact, he was born in 1964. It was as if he was in limbo and couldn't become an official person until he was adopted. But he assumed the wrong dates were just a clerical error. Darryl also remembers all these little "cousins" about his age who would stay for a while, then disappear. His parents were providing a foster home for these children, and Darryl was one of them. One of his earliest memories was of two women coming to the door to collect one of the other children, Oscar. One of the ladies was Oscar's mother, and the other was a social worker. Darryl kept trying to peek through his father's legs to find out what was happening, but his mother kept blocking him.

"I still don't know why, of all those kids, they chose me to be their son," Darryl told me. "That's a conversation I should have with my adoptive mother very soon."

A close friend who felt sorry for him and was trying to be protective managed to convince Darryl that he looked a little like his mom, and the kids from the neighborhood eased up on the adoption jokes. But the doubts remained, especially when Darryl hit puberty and his genetics kicked in. He shot up to six one. He was all muscle, towering over his mom and dad.

But by then, he was breezing through one of the top colleges in the city, St. John's University, and his rap career was already revving up. He went from success to success. Run–DMC became the first rap group to go platinum, the first to get into movies, the first to cross over into mainstream music, the first to be inducted into the Rock and Roll Hall of Fame. He had money, success, and a beautiful family. He should have been riding high. But instead, he was miserable. He was drinking hard. He was having vocal problems and creative differences with the other members of his group. None of the trappings of success mattered to him anymore. By 1997, it'd reached a crisis point. He was touring in Asia and Africa after a remix put his group back on the top of the charts. The money was rolling in. And yet he found himself alone in his hotel room, contemplating suicide. "I was a wreck. I was asking myself, am I really here on this earth to be DMC? It doesn't get much better than that. I had everything. But none of it was fulfilling. I'd reached a point where I thought, Is this it? It felt like I was in a void," he recalled.

HITTING BOTTOM

He figured his career with Run–DMC had reached the pinnacle and after that there would be nothing more. He'd done all he could do on this earth, and he wanted to end it all to attain the next level, whatever that might be. "My stupid ass needed to leave now, to get up onto the next plane of existence," he said.

When he wasn't numbing the pain with alcohol, he was reading the Bible and building up a library of metaphysical books. Deepak Chopra didn't help. The Dalai Lama's teachings didn't make him see the point of his existence. Death was the next-best option. He went so far down that road, he even thought about exactly how he was going to kill himself. Pills? Poison? A gunshot to the head? He got in his car to drive somewhere, anywhere, maybe even over a cliff. "All I could think of was checking out of here," he recalled.

Then one night, driving home after a gig, he turned on the radio and heard Sarah McLachlan's song "Angel." Something about the lyrics—"Fly away from here/From this dark cold hotel room . . . There's vultures and thieves at your back/And the storm keeps on twisting"—caught him. The song took him back from the edge. Darryl may be a hardcore rapper, but he has a heart and soul of pure mush. He played that record every day for the next year, and Darryl swears it's what kept him from ending it all. It made him feel less alone. Something about the sadness in McLachlan's voice and the notes on the piano expressed an emptiness he felt but couldn't explain until a few years later.

He marched on, but there was more sadness to come. One

of his oldest friends and Run–DMC group mates, Jam Master Jay, was killed in October 2002. A few months later, in 2003, Darryl's father died. It was a tragic ending to life as he knew it. Now, more than ever, he needed to search.

Slowly, Darryl brought himself back from the edge of the abyss. He got sober and started working out and eating right. Today, he's a total health nut. When life gets to him, he hits the weights instead of getting high. He also started on a process of self-discovery by researching and writing his memoir. But it became something much bigger when he learned he was adopted. By then, he'd embarked on an epic existential journey. "I think my spirit was crying out to say, *This is who I really am.*" But he couldn't square his public image with how he felt about himself. "Everything that was known about me was in music and on TV, but there was a whole part of my existence even I didn't know about."

Darryl has an uncanny ability to distill a profound emotion into a single phrase that says it all. When his mother and brother Alfred questioned his motives for wanting to find his birth mother, he told them, "All I am trying to do is to become who I am. Success without significance means nothing."

There's a first chapter in everybody's life, and Darryl knew he needed to get back there and discover his origins in order to understand where to go from there. His adoptive mother was sick, and his brother Alfred blamed Darryl and his quest to find his birth mother for making her sicker. But Darryl persisted, despite the guilt trips. He thought that making his story public in a documentary and filming his search would also be therapeutic for millions of other adoptees who felt isolated and needed support. But it was much more than that. For him, the adoption journey wasn't just about finding his birth parents. It was about finding himself. On camera, he said, "It's a release for me, but what my mother doesn't understand is that it can be a release for her, too. My love for her won't change. She doesn't have to fear this."

MY NAME IS . . .

When adoptees begin their search, they shouldn't make any assumptions that the facts they are told about their birth are completely accurate. They need to verify, verify, verify. It's not that adoptive parents intentionally deceive, but memories fade and facts get distorted.

Darryl wanted confirmation that his birth name was, in fact, Darryl Lovelace. His wife, Zuri, was anxious to know if Darryl really was his birth name. They'd named their son Darryl, and it mattered somehow that it was the name he'd started out in life with. It would also make the search that much easier. Darryl's next step was to go to the New York Public Library and pull out the big book of names for all births in the five boroughs that took place in 1964. He needed to eyeball his name in black and white. And there it was: Darryl Lovelace. He was so excited, he even made up a cocky little rhyme, bebopping down the library hall: "Darryl Lovelace is in the place/With the pace, in your face . . ."

But reality was also starting to hit home. Darryl stayed up all that night, running this new/old name and identity through his brain and letting it sink in. All that he knew about his existence was starting to shift. Nothing was quite the same anymore. It suddenly occurred to him that if he'd never been adopted and he'd kept the name Lovelace, he never would have had his famous rap moniker, and the whole course of hip-hop history might have been very different. "I couldn't have been DMC!"

Now that he had a name, he wanted his birth certificate. When you're adopted, a piece of physical evidence that you were born on such and such a day means everything. It's validation on so many levels. His next stop was New York's Bureau of Vital Records. That proved to be a dead end. Only his "official" adoptive birth certificate would be released, and it wasn't filed under his original birth name. All it told him was that he had been born in Harlem Hospital, not in Brooklyn as he'd originally thought. He pushed and pushed to get the original birth certificate. But he was told in no uncertain terms that the record would be sealed forever. He'd never get his hands on it.

By now, Darryl was getting frustrated, and angry. He had the feeling that everybody was against him in this quest—his family, the State of New York, the universe. Years later, he wrote a rap lyric about what he was going through; it perfectly sums up what we all feel as adoptees bumping up against the bureaucracy of a closed adoption:

> At night I can't sleep, I toss and turn
> My true reality is what I wanna learn
> But they are tellin' me I can't see the proof
> On a little piece of paper that holds the truth

He started seeing a psychiatrist and he stepped up his attendance at adoption support groups. It was the first time he didn't feel totally alone in this. The people he met in these groups encouraged him to keep going. They'd all been through it. They understood better than anyone that discovering your origins is a way to start the grieving process for the loss of your birth parents. They totally identified with Darryl's confusion and fear. Here was this big secret you were never supposed to know—that you're born as this other person, with this whole other identity and family history. "My mother thinks I'm being selfish," he told them. "Yes, I am being selfish. And for good reason. I want to find out who I am!"

It wasn't much to start with. All he had was the information listed on the official "vault copy" of his birth certificate: his mother's age, his birth date, and the fact that he had been born in Harlem Hospital. Darryl was running around in circles. He went back to Wendy to ask her how he could get his hands on the original paperwork. "Oh, that's never going to happen," she said. But Wendy did guide Darryl one step closer to his goal when she put him in touch with me.

GETTING REAL

It was around Halloween 2005 when he first showed up at my house in New Jersey. I could tell he was as nervous as I was. This is a guy who usually eats clean, but he kept scooping handfuls of chocolate from the candy bowl I had in the hallway, stuffing them in his pockets when he thought no one was looking. We sat down in my office to review the information he'd gathered together. He kept saying, "I can't believe I'm doing this." It was almost as if he were trying to pull off a heist and someone was about to bust in on him. I told him to keep going.

"You're really, really doing this," I told him. "No one ever regrets searching. Even though it didn't turn out the way I'd hoped when I found my birth parents, I'd do it a million times over, because I needed to know." It was the first time I'd shared my story with him, and I could see the tension melt off his face when he knew he was in the company of someone who truly understood. At one point, I thought Darryl was going to move in, he felt so at home, and I would have let him.

But there was work to do. We had an alleged name, but it wasn't consistent with someone from the Dominican Republic. If she was from the DR, I prayed the birth mother hadn't moved back there in the interim. That would make the search incredibly complicated. We agreed he should go back to where it all started, Harlem Hospital, and ask for his birth records. It might get sticky. They might ask for his ID, and obviously he didn't have ID that said "Darryl Lovelace" on it. There was a chance he might get stonewalled again. Darryl was getting nervous. "Oh

no! I think I need cookies and ice cream. I need comfort food!"
he said. I guess that was another thing we had in common—a
sweet-tooth reaction to stress.

Darryl decided to hang out for a while when he found out
my two boys were into music. One of my little guys plays bass,
and the other is a guitarist, and at all hours of the day they
practice so hard, I can feel the floor and walls of my home office
throbbing. My kids treated this music icon to an impromptu
jam session in our garage while Darryl rhymed off their beats.
Then he sat them down in all earnestness and told them that if
they wanted to pursue music careers, they'd better stay away
from drugs and cursing. It turns out he's not a fan of today's
hardcore hip-hop. He's an old-school rapper who's all about the
social message. I wasn't necessarily in awe of who he was as part
of Run–DMC, but in that moment I was overwhelmed with
admiration for who he is now, as a person. Honestly, I adore the
man.

He came back two or three more times to discuss the case,
and each time he'd wind up listening to rock with my boys,
watching videos, and eating. I'll never forget that night my
mother and I cooked one of our big Italian meals. There was a
Giants game on, and my mother and all the boys sat on the
couch together to watch. Mike, my two sons, my mother, and
Darryl were squished up together on the sofa. There they were,
their heads in a row, bobbing up and down in excitement and
shouting at the television screen when their team scored a
touchdown.

Darryl is always welcome in my home. In fact, he's become a
huge fan of my turkey meatballs, just as I have become a huge
fan of his music.

The day after his first chat with me, he went straight to
Harlem Hospital, cameras in tow. He spoke to the young guy
behind a glass partition in the records office, who clearly knew
who Darryl was. And naturally he was in awe. But he had to do

his job and ask Darryl for some ID showing that he was Darryl Lovelace.

"Nah, sorry, I got nothin' on me. Nothin' that says who I am," he told the guy.

"I really need to see some ID."

"Nope, nothin'. Well, unless you count my album cover."

That was it. The young man laughed in spite of himself. He was so bowled over by Darryl's charm, he took him into a conference room and opened up the 1964 book of birth records to the relevant page. Just at that moment, a senior hospital official walked in and told Darryl he couldn't see the documents until he produced some legitimate ID. She was a formidable woman. There was no arguing with her. Darryl walked away graciously, but not before he had a chance to eyeball two pieces of information that would be pivotal to his search: his birth mom's actual name—Berncenia Lovelace—and a Harlem address where she was living at the time Darryl was born. Darryl swung by his new friend's cubbyhole to double-check the spelling of the name he'd only had the opportunity to glance at, and again the kid did him a favor and spelled it out. Then they gave each other a fist pump through the glass partition. It was Darryl's first big victory against the adoption bureaucracy, and he was psyched!

He called me immediately with the good news. I told him to check out the neighborhood but to be careful. If she was still there, he couldn't just go knocking on doors and scare her away or make her feel her privacy was threatened. He needed to take a gentler approach. Darryl walked around the streets, already empathizing with the mother he'd never met. "I can feel the pressure of what she was feeling when she was walking around here with me in her belly," he told me.

Darryl and his producer went to the address he'd seen on the hospital document—Hamilton Terrace—and his producer buzzed the apartment. The tenant inside let them in, and the producer ran upstairs to knock on the door. Darryl waited downstairs and overheard the conversation his producer had with an elderly woman. "Hi, we're looking for a Berncenia Lovelace, who was living here in 1964. Did you know her?

"Berncenia from Staten Island? Yes! That's my niece!"

Darryl got chills. He couldn't believe that a family member still lived in the building, forty years later. Technically, the woman upstairs was his great-aunt. But before he had the chance to follow his impulse and bound up the stairs to give her a hug, the conversation was cut short. Her nephew ordered her to shut the door. "We don't know what this about," he told her.

Darryl was jubilant. Finally, he was getting closer to the truth. But he didn't know the half of it. I'd already done a little snooping and had run Berncenia's name through a database of all the names of people presently living in the United States. There was only one Berncenia Lovelace in the whole country. The listing even included her current address and phone number in Staten Island. I didn't tell him what I'd found. I just told him to come right over.

He picked up his wife, then rushed over to my house. I explained what I'd done, and showed him what I'd found. "So guess who I think we're looking at."

"My mother? That's crazy!"

"This is it. This information is as current as you can get."

"For real?"

"Yup. So the question is, What are you going to do next?"

"That's a good question!"

Now it was real. Darryl's first contact with his birth mother was a letter or a phone call away. My personal preference is a phone call. Other people in my business advocate writing a letter. They contend that sending something through the mail is less intrusive and shocking. But letters can end up in the wrong hands. There's less control. With a phone call, you can understand the person you are talking to immediately. It takes a lot of the stress away because it expedites the contact. A letter creates more anxiety on both sides. When you send someone a letter, it's like saying, *Not only do I know who you are; I know where you live.* And for the sender, there's the question of what comes next. What if there's no response? What if the letter never got there? The person on the other end could be on vacation and away for three weeks. Then you torment yourself. When you are waiting for a response to a world-rocking letter like that, it can seem like a lifetime. But it's up to my clients. I'll guide and support them, but it's their decision.

SNAIL MAIL

Darryl opted for a letter. He drove into Manhattan, went to a stationery store on Fifth Avenue called Jam, and bought a stack of bright green stationery. He sat in his car, writing, crumpling, and discarding several versions of his handwritten note. He finally settled on something simple: "Hi, I have reason to believe that I am your son. Please call. Love, Darryl."

Days later, a reply to his letter still hadn't come. Darryl was beside himself. He felt like he was being rejected all over again. He was having panic attacks. At night, he couldn't breathe. He had insomnia, tossing and turning all night with the same two words running in his mind: *What if, what if, what if . . .*

By week two, he was a total mess. His emotions were manifested in all kinds of physical symptoms. He had stomach pain, back pain, and headaches. He was on two kinds of powerful pain meds. He'd swing from fear that his birth mother would take one look at his letter and throw it away to anger at the possibility that his relationship with her was being denied. "It makes me want to drive it into her skull that I AM YOUR SON!" he said.

This was about acceptance. He desperately needed her acknowledgment. He toyed with the idea of driving to her house, walking in, and throwing his arms around her, whether she was happy to see him or not. He wanted to tell her, *You don't have to be ashamed. You didn't just throw me away. You gave me a chance to have a wonderful life. Look at me!*

Finally, he got something in the mail. It was the letter he'd sent, stamped "Return to sender." His birth mother had never gotten it. It just so happened that on the day it arrived, there was a different mail-delivery person on duty, and he didn't realize the Berncenia who'd lived at that address for decades was listed under both a married name and a maiden name. The substitute mailman didn't recognize the last name and assumed this was the wrong person. Darryl was ecstatic. It meant there was still hope that she wanted to see him.

When he got the returned letter, he hightailed it over to my place with his wife, Zuri, in tow. Darryl knew it was time to step up and make the call, but he needed to do it from a place where he felt he had plenty of support. The poor guy was all nerves, rehearsing what he was going to say over and over again. Zuri and I sat across the table from him while he dithered. He was losing courage, and thinking he might just send another letter. I slid the phone in his direction and said, "No more letters, Darryl. This time, you gotta just do it!"

"I need a meeting with Adoptions Anonymous," he said.

"You can have a meeting in a couple of days. First you have to call."

"What do I say?"

"Go with your heart!"

He dialed the number and she picked up on the first ring. "Hello?"

"Good evening. Can I speak to Berncenia, please?"

"Speaking."

"How are you doing? This is Darryl Lovelace."

"Who?"

"My name is Darryl Lovelace. I am hoping you can help me.

I am looking for my birth mother, and I have reason to believe you may be she."

"Really? When were you born?"

"May 31, 1964, in Harlem Hospital."

"Okay, um, it's possible."

There was a lengthy pause. She didn't sound shocked or upset to hear from him so much as perplexed. Then Darryl broke the silence. "I am sitting here with my wife, because this is the hardest thing I've ever done. . . ."

"How did you find me?"

"Oh, it's a long, long story. I'd love to meet with you to tell you about the journey. The way my life has been going has been incredible, and you are a part of the blessing that is my life."

"Oh wow!"

"I would love to meet you in person."

"Oh! That would be nice!"

"Wow, really? That's so incredible!"

"What did you think? That I was going to say no?"

"Nooo! I didn't know what to think! This is so incredible. I don't know what to think! I don't even know what to say right now. Wow! This just happened!"

"So how are we going to arrange it?"

"Um, um . . . I could come tomorrow!"

"Okay, I'll be ready for you at one o'clock."

Meanwhile, Zuri was whispering to Darryl to thank his birth mother, and giving him the thumbs-up. I couldn't believe how well it was going. This woman was so pleasant and laid-back, considering she'd just heard from the son she'd given up four decades ago.

"You are part of something amazing, I am telling you. Thank you! Thank you so much. I don't know what to say except thank you!"

"Well, I am looking forward to this."

"Thank you!"

".You're welcome!"

Darryl was beside himself when he got off the phone. Miracles do happen!

No one told Berncenia who Darryl was. We didn't want her to know he was a celebrity. We wanted her desire to meet him to come from a place of authenticity. But I suspected that someone, like her aunt at Hamilton Terrace, had tipped her off that she'd be getting a call. They didn't know who Darryl was, but his visit had raised a few flags. Or maybe Berncenia had an intuition. She seemed too calm and collected for someone who'd been caught off guard. Weeks later, Berncenia wrote me a beautiful letter, telling me how grateful she was that Darryl had found her, and revealing exactly what was going on inside her head at the time of the phone call. It explained everything.

I wasn't as calm as Darryl thought I was. Like him, I couldn't breathe. My "Inner Child" (the voice in my head) was telling me to "Breathe, Breathe." There were lots of thoughts playing and replaying in my head. I was also dealing with my "Inner Child" yelling at me for saying, "It's possible." "It's possible"? You know he's your son. Why did you say that? That's the dumbest thing you've ever said! He's talking to you now. Answer him, say something! But, it all went well. It was Real. You probably don't know, when I spoke to Darryl (Lovelace) the second time he told me he was a musician. I asked him if he played an instrument, he said no he sang and had a few albums out. I was thinking, but didn't say, "If you stick with it, maybe you'll make it." Surprise, surprise.

The story of how she came to give Darryl up for adoption was like that of so many birth mothers. She was young, poor, and dependent upon her family for survival. She grew up in Hamilton Heights, Harlem, and when her father announced they were going to relocate to Staten Island to get away from the city, she was devastated. She had to leave behind all her friends, her boyfriend, and the life she knew. She was forbidden to go back there, but at every opportunity she'd sneak off to be with her old boyfriend. At eighteen, he got her pregnant with Darryl's half brother, Mark. Her parents agreed to let her keep the baby, and Mark was raised by Berncenia's aunt. These were the people Darryl had surprised earlier with his impromptu visit. Berncenia continued to run around the streets of Harlem. She was a tall, striking woman with a will of her own, and she fell in love with another man, Darryl's father. But when, at twenty-one, she became pregnant a second time, her parents weren't having any of it. "Hell no, not another one," her father said. "We cannot do this again." This child, Darryl, would have to be given up for adoption.

SHARED DNA

Of course, Darryl would discover all of this as he got to know his birth mom. But first, he had to meet her. The day after the call, Darryl made the trek to Berncenia's apartment on Staten Island. He took along his wife and his young son, who carried a huge bunch of peach-colored roses for his birth grandmother. Berncenia was ready for them at the door, smiling and laughing. She opened her arms wide and gave Darryl the kind of huge bear hug he's always giving to other people. You could see the resemblance right away: tall, athletic, with a kind open face and huge eyes. It was his DNA all right.

Darryl's career was a surprise. Berncenia had always imagined her son was a lawyer, not a hip-hop icon.

"I don't know how you'd put rappers and lawyers together," Darryl commented. "Maybe because we have a lot to say?"

It wasn't just their looks that were similar. When Darryl

walked into Berncenia's living room, he saw the same Buddhist statue he had in his living room. On her bookshelves was the same extensive collection of metaphysical books. On his right arm is tattooed the word *Zuri*, which is not only the name of his wife; it's also the Swahili word for "beautiful." On Berncenia's right arm is a tattoo of the Peruvian symbol for "beautiful." Like Darryl, Berncenia is soft-spoken, highly intelligent, worldly, yet down-to-earth.

"When I look at her, I finally see me," he said.

There could have been no better result than this. I was so relieved for Darryl. It was like they'd known each other their whole lives. They got each other. They had the same sense of humor and ready smile. As he sat on the sofa in her tidy little apartment, he held her hand and said, "You and my mother, the both of y'all, I don't look at you as two separate people. I look at you as one entity of motherhood and love."

Darryl sees the combination of the two women as the reason for his success in life. Berncenia brought him into the world and passed along much of his creative and spiritual side. But his adoptive mother—in fact, his whole adoptive family—got him to where he needed to go. They taught him how to operate in this life, and gave him the values that make him the special person he is today.

"Would I have loved to have been with my birth mother this whole time? Sure! But that wasn't part of the whole plan. I needed both," he said.

As for Berncenia, she was genuinely surprised to find out who her son was. It never occurred to her that he could be this big celebrity. But, she said, she always felt a bond. "I knew you would come," she told him. "I felt all along that we were spiritually connected."

When the documentary cameras weren't rolling, Berncenia had a lot more to say to Darryl, but she was getting concerned that he seemed too composed. At one point, she broke off the conversation to ask, "Are you mad? Do you want to scream at me?"

"Huh? No!"

Berncenia was convinced there had to be some blame and anger lurking beneath Darryl's sweet exterior. She felt she deserved it, for giving him up, and she was bracing herself. Four more times she asked him, "Is today the day?" She wanted him to let his emotions out. But as much as Darryl searched for his anger, it wasn't there.

"I've got no reason to be angry. She did what she did to give me a chance in life. I have everything I ever needed."

Soon after, Darryl met his three siblings, including his older brother, Mark. A few years after Berncenia gave up Darryl, she met a man who fathered his younger brother and sister. They all got together for Thanksgiving dinner and had a big family reunion. Darryl went from not looking like anybody in his family to seeing his face in the people all around him. For him, it was heaven.

ENOUGH ALREADY!

Today, Darryl sees his birth mother regularly. But nothing has changed with his adoptive family. He immediately wrote his mother and Alfred a letter, telling them how much he loved them both and saying nothing had changed. They were still his family.

A couple of weeks after his reunion with his birth family, he started visiting his adoptive mother more often. He took her to breakfast on Monday, and then he went back to Queens on Wednesday and took her to lunch. On Friday, he took her out for dinner at a Chinese restaurant. He just sat there, watching her eat. Finally, his mom put her fork down, looked up at him, and said, "Darryl, I don't want to see your ass again."

"Huh?"

"I know. I know you love me. I get it. Thank you."

She knew what he was doing and that he wanted to demonstrate how much he still loved her by spending so much time with her. It was her way of saying he didn't have to feel guilty anymore and that everything was fine between them. He could go on with his life. Finding his birth mother actually came as a relief to his adoptive mother. It was the fear of the unknown that was torturing her, but the reality of it wasn't so bad. It was making her son happy, and bringing him closer to her. When he told her, it was like watching a cloud lift.

Not knowing causes emotional pain for the whole adoption triad: the birth parents, the adoptive family, and, most of all, the adoptee. But Darryl understands that just as it's not his birth mother's fault—circumstances left her no choice—the secrecy, shame, and fear that adoptive parents feel are also unwarranted. It's why the facts of an adoptee's existence should not be kept hidden. Darryl even made another rhyme about it: "If you remove the guilt and pain, you remove the shame."

Darryl's adoption story is far from over. That initial reunion was just the beginning. He continues to have a great relationship with his birth family. Berncenia refers to herself as Darryl's "other mother," and she and his adoptive mother have indicated a willingness to meet, although it hasn't happened yet. But he still struggles over which family he is going to spend the holidays with, and he'd like nothing more than to bring both families together one Christmas in the near future.

Then there is the question of whether or not to reunite with his birth father. A few days after Darryl found Berncenia, she happened to see his father on the street. She was on a bus, going home after work, but she jumped off at the next stop and went back to the stoop where he was sitting. He was drinking something out of a paper bag.

"Do you remember me telling you that you have a son out there?" she ventured to ask him.

"Yeah. So?"

"Well, I found him."

"Whateva. I don't care about no kids."

Berncenia didn't say who Darryl was. She remembered reading a story about an NBA star's birth father turning up with his hand out, and she didn't want her son to have the same experience. But she decided to take a picture of him, just so that Darryl would have the opportunity to see what he looked like. She snapped him quickly on her camera phone. But as she was walking away, she realized he had his sunglasses on. She walked back and asked him for a retake.

"Hell no!" he said.

"Aw, come on. Take your sunglasses off. Just one."

"Okay, just one. Take it or leave it."

Her camera was just about to die, but she got the shot. When she showed Darryl, he didn't see much of a resemblance. But their hands were identical. For now, he has no real desire to meet his father. He's been warned that the man is not a loving kind of guy. He has a daughter in Atlanta and they have no relationship, either. But Darryl knows where he is. Like his birth mother, his birth father is rooted in Staten Island, and he's been living at the same address for decades. Barring death, insanity, or incarceration, he's not going anywhere anytime soon.

I recently urged Darryl to reach out to him for no other reason than that he has a right to know about his medical history. He owes it to himself and his own children. He plans to do it before his father goes to his grave, but he's not ready yet.

"I don't have that same spark I had to find my birth mother," he told me. "Besides, I'm still getting to know her, and all my other birth relatives. It's been six years, but that's not long enough to catch up on a lifetime. I just want to enjoy having them in my life."

MAN ON A MISSION

Even if his adoption story hadn't turned out as well as it did, Darryl is convinced he'd want to know, because it would be *his* truth. "If I was left in a phone booth, that's still my story. If my mother was raped, that's my story. Then it would be my mission in life to help rape victims."

His journey has helped him retool his sense of purpose. A few weeks after his reunion, Darryl got together with his musical idol, Sarah McLachlan, to collaborate on the Harry Chapin classic "Cat's in the Cradle." Darryl decided to do a remix of the song, changing it from a song about regret to an uplifting one for adopted and foster children everywhere. "Just Like Me" captures the experience so perfectly, it could be an anthem for the search:

I have a lot of thoughts like who the hell am I
What is the truth and what is a lie?
But I think about my life and everything is okay
I gotta pave the way to a brighter day

Being adopted and experiencing that burning desire to know makes you a member of a very special club. It doesn't matter who you are, or where you're from. You could be a housewife and a mom in New Jersey, or a rap icon. Anyone. When you find out that another person is adopted, you understand them on a whole new level, because you've shared the same emotions at one time or another. When Sarah and Darryl were in the studio recording that song together, she looked him in the eye and said, "Darryl, I was adopted, too."

Ever since his documentary aired, he's connected with thousands of kids who felt exactly the same way he did, he says. "Every time I go back to the hood, foster kids come up to me and say, 'Mr. DMC, thank you for putting it out there, because I felt so alone.'"

The whole experience has turned him into an advocate for thousands of kids. He got together with Sheila Jaffe to start Felix. Named after an imaginary dog who was adopted by a family of cats, the organization set up a camp where foster children can form a bond with one another. Darryl is very hands-on. He's been directly involved in helping hundreds of children from New York City go to summer camp upstate for three weeks. The interlude gives them an opportunity to find love and support from those who understand what they're going through. That's the Felix organization's whole mission, and other celebrities are catching on to its importance. Actor Mark Wahlberg has been a generous donor to the cause, and former *Sopranos* star Lorraine Bracco is the honorary chairwoman.

"We were lucky. We got taken home. We want to give back to those who didn't get taken home," says Darryl.

He's also become a strong advocate for open adoptions. He's pushing New York State to change its laws about sealed birth records. "Who does the government think they're protecting? If we deal with the issues of our existence in an honest way, the world would be a better place," Darryl says. "It's disrespectful that we can't know where we came from. This institutionalized secrecy is wrong!"

I'm not an activist, but I'm with Darryl. It should be a human right to know how you came to be on this earth. The Catholic Church, on some false moralistic grounds, is one of the groups most opposed to opening up the records. Whenever I've dealt with priests and nuns on my searches over the years, I've always reminded them that religion is based on truth, not lies. After all, even Moses was adopted, and we know how important it was for him to find out his true identity. Understanding where he came from gave him the power to change the world.

"Ours is the story of purpose and destiny," says Darryl. Once he gets on this subject, there's no stopping him. I love that about him. When he accepted his Emmy for making the documentary about his adoption, he made this promise: "For my fellow adoptees, I am going to remove the guilt and the shame from the triad of birth mom, adoptee, and adopted parents, and thus will remove the pain. If you thought this documentary changed a multitude of lives, my next project will change lives again, change laws, change history, and change the world!"

For Darryl, the search became an awakening of sorts. It brought him renewed energy and focus, both as a man and as an artist. But it didn't change who he was. Finding his birth mother gave him self-acceptance and the confidence to move forward in his life. But he was, is, and always will be the same person. Darryl says it best: "You are who you are, and all you have to do is just love each other."

The Lesson: We Are All Connected

There is a sisterhood and brotherhood of adoptees that can open up your world. This is a lesson that comes from DMC himself, and one I learned in the process of doing the documentary with him. I'd been working from home and was starting to become somewhat distanced from the rest of the world. But being a part of filming the documentary caused me to come out of my shell in a way that didn't allow me to remain unengaged. I met this man who was famous and had every reason to be uninterested in my little life. But he made me feel welcome, appreciated, and a part of something really special.

I connected to him on a level that I never expected. We bonded in a way that only people who've been through some kind of trauma can. You think others won't understand, but there are people out there who really do get it, and that's empowering. It gives you strength to know that you are not alone in your experience.

Even though I don't speak to Darryl every day, I would like to think that he knows my love for him as a friend is true. I would do anything for him. He's family.

CHAPTER FIVE

Close to Home

◆ ◆ ◆

It was the deep dark secret in my family. None of my cousins knew. My aunts and uncles never discussed it. I had no idea. So when my mother asked me to do a favor for my favorite cousin, Joanne Montenegro, I was blown away. All those years I'd been obsessing about my own adoption journey and yet this dear woman, whom I call Aunt Joanne, had been suffering in silence, never able to find real happiness since she was forced by her father to give up her son for adoption forty-four years earlier.

Equally surprising was the fact that it was Mom who asked me to find Aunt Joanne's son. I'd already been involved in the search game for ten years, and I guess my mother was sufficiently impressed. She'd moved into our home in South Jersey a couple of years earlier, so she got to see up close what I do for a living, and how I do it. She saw the positive effect my work was having on my clients, and me, and I think she was finally accepting the idea of a search. It still bothered her plenty that I ever looked for or tried to build any kind of connection with my own birth relatives, but, as for the rest of the world, she got it. She was proud of her baby girl.

Mom was working her usual magic in the kitchen, whipping up some meatballs and gravy for my hungry kids, when she laid on the bombshell. "Pammie honey, I need you to do something for your aunt Joanne, but I need you to do it quietly."

"What is it, Mom?"

"She has a son. She wasn't allowed to keep him, and I know she's never gotten over it. I'd like you to try to find him. But you have to do it in a way that looks like an accident. Joanne can't know that you and I had this conversation. *Capisce?* I can't have her thinking that I betrayed her confidence."

"Whoa! Mom, you're just telling me this now?"

She shrugged and went back to stirring the sauce pot on the stove. "I guess it's just time," she said. "Joanne deserves to be happy."

I thought back to my childhood and all those times I'd spent with Aunt Joanne. She was a few years younger than Mom, but they were best friends and she was always at our house. Technically, she wasn't my aunt. She was my second cousin on my father's side of the family. We come from a huge Italian family on Long Island, and all the cousins, aunts, and uncles were really close and always in and out of one another's houses. My grandma Rosie and her family had an Italian restaurant in Corona, Queens, called Ferrara's. It doesn't exist anymore, but we ate there every week. Our entire clan was always at the restaurant, either working or eating, including Joanne, who worked there as a waitress. I'd always have some aunt stuffing food in my mouth, pinching my cheeks, and shoving a few dollars in my pocket. They'd feed you until you wanted to throw up. Then we'd go to the pastry stop next door. It was heaven!

But the one relative who always made me and my brother Ronnie feel special was Aunt Joanne. To my young eyes, she was this glamour queen. She looked like a young Sophia Loren, and she had a way of speaking to me, like a little adult, that made me feel as if I belonged and could do anything. Not that my parents didn't love me and support me, but having that extra acceptance and encouragement from an adult in your life whom you admire is a big deal when you're a kid. I always felt a bit like the odd one out when I was growing up. Again, I always knew my brother and I were adopted, and we were proud of that fact, but we were the only members of the family who weren't blood. Joanne always took the trouble to make us feel like we were a part of her tribe. It went a long way.

Looking back, I realize she was paying special attention to us because, in a way, she was hoping that her own child was receiving the same love and acceptance in *his* adoptive family. It wasn't necessarily a conscious impulse on her part. But when I asked her later if that was the case, she thought about it for a minute, and said, "It makes sense. When I saw you, I'd always think about my own child. I couldn't offer him any of the love and attention I wanted to give him, so I guess I was giving it to you. But you were always special to me."

As kind as she was, there was a palpable sadness about my aunt Joanne. And now I understand why. Joanne grew up in a strict household. Her father, my uncle Frankie, was basically a good man, or at least he did what he thought was the right thing by his family. But everyone was afraid of him. It wasn't unusual for the time that Uncle Frankie believed Italians married Italians, no exceptions, but his intolerance was extreme. He didn't care if his bigotry cost his daughter her happiness, and Joanne's mom didn't dare call him on it. What he said was law, and no one, not even my dad, would question or defy him.

WEST SIDE STORY

As a teenager, Joanne used to run around with a group of kids from the neighborhood. Pretty soon, she fell in love with a boy in her crew named Ruben, a tall and handsome Puerto Rican from a good family. But it was a real *West Side Story*/*Romeo and Juliet* scenario. There was a lot of prejudice. Uncle Frankie tended to view everyone in that community as a "dirty immigrant." There was no way he was going to let a daughter of his associate with a Puerto Rican, much less date or marry one. But Joanne was madly in love. They sneaked around together for the next three years. Joanne knew it was forbidden. Then the inevitable happened: She got pregnant. By that time, Ruben was nineteen, and Joanne was eighteen. Legally, they were both adults, but running off together at the time seemed out of the question. Joanne was terrified of her father, and so was Ruben.

The day came when Joanne had to admit to her parents what had happened. She was three months pregnant and she was showing. Of course, Uncle Frankie hit the roof. He called her every nasty name in the book. She told him that Ruben wanted to be with her and he'd do the right thing, but her dad's only response was, "There will be no illegitimate babies in this house!"

I'm not sure if it would have made a difference what the ethnic background of the baby was. My uncle viewed this as an embarrassment for the family. Immediately, she was sent away. Had she followed her heart, she would have been ostracized from the entire Montenegro family. Her older sister happened to be pregnant at the same time as Joanne. But she was married. She told Uncle Frankie she'd be happy to take them both in and, publicly at least, raise Joanne's baby as her own. But he told her in no uncertain terms that she would also be ostracized if she dared to interfere. The decision was made.

WHAT COULD'VE BEEN

This was 1960, four years before I was born and adopted into my family. And the kicker was that my parents were looking to adopt at the time. If they'd fully understood what was happening to Joanne, I don't doubt they'd have stepped up and offered to raise her baby, too. But it was too late. She'd already been sent away to a home for unwed mothers in Brooklyn.

Of course, Aunt Joanne still tortures herself with all the

what-ifs. "Maybe if I'd called my father's bluff, this wouldn't have happened. I don't know. My father was a good man. He tried to do right, but as far as he was concerned, I brought shame to the family. I could only marry an Italian. If I defied him, I wouldn't be allowed to come home. What could I do?"

She broke off all contact with Ruben. She was afraid of what might happen to him if Uncle Frankie found out they'd been in contact. No one could talk to her dad. She spent the next six months hidden away at the Angel Guardian Home with dozens of other pregnant girls waiting to give birth and give up their children. It's not that the nuns were unkind, but she was kept under lock and key in that virtual prison. There were bars on the windows. She couldn't come and go as she pleased, for fear a neighbor or friend might see her and recognize her. Her father never even came to visit. Occasionally, her mother and sister would sneak away and keep her company. But she was basically alone in that depressing house, and about to undergo the most traumatic experience of her life, with no one to hold her hand and comfort her.

When the time came, the nuns rushed her to Maimonides Hospital. It was a long, hard labor. Her baby weighed eight pounds, seven ounces. She named him Michael. Aunt Joanne still remembers vividly what he looked like as a baby. "He was a little butterball. Perfect in every way. He was brought to me for a few minutes while I was lying in recovery. It was the only time I was allowed to hold him. I overheard the head nurse order the rest of the hospital staff not to bring the baby to me again because he was going to be given up for adoption. But as soon as I could get up, I walked over to the nursery. I stood there for as long as I could and stared at him through the glass partition. I memorized his little face, those ten tiny fingers and toes. I went there every day for the next five days I was in the hospital."

She stayed at the Angel Guardian a few more weeks, while her body healed. They kept baby Michael downstairs in the crib room with all the other babies. It was hard for Joanne to know he was there and that she couldn't see him. And life didn't get much better when she was finally allowed to return home to Queens. No one dared mention the baby. The whole topic was taboo. Everyone acted as if it had never happened.

And yet the reminders for Joanne were constant. Her sister had her baby three weeks after Joanne had given birth, and everyone celebrated this new addition to the Montenegro family. Joanne was happy for her sister, and her sister was heartbroken over what had happened to Joanne, but seeing her baby niece all the time must have felt like an extra twist of the knife.

It didn't get much better. The marriage to her first husband was not a happy one. I remember him well. He was this incredibly handsome man—Italian, of course. I used to hide under the bed or behind the sofa when they came over, because he always tried to grab me and give me a big kiss. It was his little joke. But he had a mean temper. On the outside, they looked like the perfect couple, but there were signs that things were very wrong. I knew that at one point my dad was going to kick his ass.

Joanne told her husband before she married him that she'd had a baby and given him up for adoption. She wasn't going to have any secrets from her husband. His response was cold: "Well, I forgive you, but I'll never forget."

"That should have been my first red flag," recalls Joanne. "Now that I think back on it, I'm pretty sure I married him just to get out of my father's house."

PAYING THE PRICE

But they stayed together for sixteen years. Joanne longed to have more kids, but after their first year together, they found out that he was sterile. She just couldn't get a break. I don't know why Joanne accepted her lot and stayed with him for so long, but low self-esteem is a common thread among birth mothers. Many of them think they don't deserve to be happy, and they go through life settling for less. Even today, with the hindsight of decades, she blames herself for what happened to her. "A lot of this was my fault. I was so afraid. Ruben kept trying to get in touch after I told him I was pregnant, and I told him I couldn't see him. Fear ruled my life," she says.

When Uncle Frankie died in 1981, Joanne made an attempt at a search for Michael. She contacted the agency that had put him up for adoption. She searched for him on the Internet. But she was going under her own last name, so of course nothing turned up. She didn't pursue it any further. As is often the case with birth mothers, she was afraid of the disappointment of not finding him, and the rejection if she did. Once again, fear paralyzed her.

The years passed. Aunt Joanne divorced her first husband and finally met a nice man, Joe, who was kind and supportive. They moved to Jupiter, Florida, bought a nice condo, and Joanne found a comfortable office job. Life was definitely on the upswing. She told Joe about Michael, and he encouraged her to find her son. That opportunity came a few years ago, when my cousins were visiting Aunt Joanne and discussed what I did for a living. We'd been out of touch, so she had no idea.

THE TENTATIVE STEP

It got her thinking. But she still didn't dare come out and ask me. She found an excuse to get in touch when she was going through her records and needed a current address for her ex-husband for some reason. She called me up and asked me for the favor, which I was only too happy to do for her, and when I mentioned to Mom that Joanne had been in touch, it must have been the trigger for her sudden revelation to me. Since Joanne was asking me to find some information anyway, we figured I had the perfect excuse to do some digging. And it was easy enough to find Michael.

I called Joanne back with the information she'd asked for. Then I said, "Hey, Aunt Joanne, I got the information you wanted, but there's something I need to ask you. While I was doing another adoption case, I came across the name Michael Montenegro. Do you happen to know if anyone in the family gave up a son? Your sister, maybe?"

She was silent for what seemed like a minute.

"No, no. I don't think so, Pammie. Not in this family."

Joanne was in shock. She told me later on that she'd actually been burning to ask me this favor as soon as she found out I was a searcher, but she didn't know how. After keeping it a secret for all these years, it was her first instinct to deny it. But the information jabbed away at her. She couldn't sleep. Finally, the next morning, she called me back.

"Pammie, he's mine."

"I knew it! Here's his phone number."

"I can't call him! What if he hangs up on me?"

"Then I'll call him!"

I tracked him down. His adopted name was pure Irish— Kevin McNeil. He was living and working in Connecticut as a state marshal. He was forty-four years old by now (this was in 2004), happily married, and had two teenage daughters. The parents who raised him were good people. His mother was Italian and his father was Irish. They adopted three boys, including Kevin, and brought them up right. All three of them are well educated and successful men who grew up in an environment with a lot of love. But Kevin's mother died in 1996, and his father passed away in 2002. He was an orphan again.

I couldn't wait to call my newfound cousin. Of course, I

didn't tell him we were related. I went through my usual dialogue in order to confirm I had the right person. But this one was sharp.

"Hello, is this Kevin McNeil?" I asked.

"Yes."

"I am hoping you can help me. I am doing research for someone who is looking for family. By any chance is your date of birth July 30, 1960?"

"Yes."

"The person I am looking for is actually adopted. I have a long list of people, but could this be you?"

"Yes."

"Were you born in Brooklyn?"

His antennae went up.

"Who are you calling for? My birth mother or my birth father?"

"Your birth mother. She's looking for you."

A first, he was reluctant. He wasn't in shock. He went into detective mode. I could hear him typing away on a keyboard as he was checking his own government database for every name and fact I was giving him. His first thought was, *Oh God, what am I getting into?* There'd been a few points in his life when he'd wondered about where he came from. He and his brothers used to joke with one another that they'd been found on their parents' doorstep. Kevin knew what his last name was at the time of his birth. When he was thirteen and his parents were out, Kevin and his brothers got into his mother's papers and he saw the correspondence between his parents and the Angel Guardian Home—typed on onionskin paper. They asked his parents if they would accept a handicapped child. He saw the words *Italian* and *Puerto Rican,* but he didn't know to whom that referred. That's all he found out. But Kevin stayed curious about his birth parents throughout his teen years.

"Sure, as a kid you wonder," he told me, especially when someone yells at you. You think to yourself, Maybe my birth parents were millionaires. Maybe they'd treat me better."

As an adult, Kevin was too busy with his life to focus on the question of who his birth parents were. Once in a while the topic would come up. His wife, Cheryl, recalls him turning to her in the car and saying, "I wonder who she was."

"Who?" She asked.

"My mother."

"So why don't you look for her?"

He'd tried a couple of times. But he was looking in the wrong place, because by the time he searched, Aunt Joanne had already moved out of state.

TOUGH CUSTOMER

But when the opportunity to find out finally presented itself, Kevin's initial reaction was to say no.

"Why not?" I asked him.

"Because I already had a mother."

"Aw, come on. What have you got to lose? I know your birth mother, and she's an amazing woman. She's dying to meet you. It would make her so happy. Give it a shot. You only live once, and your life will be richer because of it."

He told me later on that he wouldn't have even considered meeting Joanne if his parents had still been alive. He thought it would have been disrespectful. His adoptive mother had been very territorial, and she would have been distraught if he'd made contact with his birth mother. A typical Italian mother, she'd loved her kids fiercely. In retrospect, it was a good thing Joanne asked me to make that first call. I can be very persuasive.

"Okay, okay. Tell her to call me. But she's got thirty seconds to do it."

Joanne got on the phone right away.

"Kevin, do you know who this is?" she asked.

"I sure do!"

He asked her all the normal questions, questions he'd always had and never known the answers to: "Why did you put me up for adoption?" "How old were you when you had me?" "Was it hard for you?" "Did you ever try to find me?" The more answers he got, the more he wanted to know.

"It was almost like a drug. I couldn't get enough," he recalled. "The questions had been bubbling up inside of me since I could remember, and now I could ask anything."

There was still some skepticism on Kevin's part. It was a law-enforcement reflex. He scoured his database as he was getting the answers from Joanne, just to see if he could catch her in a lie.

"I didn't think the whole thing was real," he admitted. "I wanted to make sure she was telling me the truth."

Joanne remembers it a little differently. She recalls that the conversation flowed naturally and easily from the moment they started talking. She told him about the circumstances of her pregnancy, and how strict her family was. Once that information came out, Kevin was immediately accepting and understanding. He asked her if she knew who his father was. She said of course she did, although she wasn't offended by the question. She was sure a lot of girls in her situation might not have known. She told him he was a good man and gave him Ruben's name. She wasn't in touch with her old boyfriend, but she'd always kept track of where he was.

MACARONI AND MEATBALLS

Kevin and Joanne—mother and son—continued talking. They sent each other file after file of JPEG pictures, their first attempt at filling in the missing years. There were so many photographs, their computers slowed down. Joanne remembers the exchange going on for about five hours.

Over the following weeks, they stayed in regular contact, but it would be another month before they could meet in person, because they lived a thousand miles apart. Aunt Joanne flew to New York to stay with her sister, and Kevin and his wife drove in from Connecticut to meet her at a Marriott Hotel on Long Island.

Joanne was so excited, she was shaking. She walked into the lobby with her husband, Joe, and asked at the front desk for Kevin. They called up to his room and told him his mother was there.

"What is she doing down there? Send her up!" he said.

Everything went into slow motion for Joanne. The elevator seemed to take forever. When she got to his floor, his room was at the end of a long corridor. She walked and walked. When she finally got to his room, the door was ajar.

She described what happened next: "His back was to me. I touched his arm. He turned around and must have hugged me for ten minutes. Cheryl, Kevin's wife, was in tears, and the whole time my husband was videotaping the scene. But to me, it was all a blur."

They went down to the coffee shop for lunch, talking endlessly. Joanne couldn't get over how tall and good-looking her son is. Their hands are identical. There is no question he is her kid. He looks a lot like his father, and although Kevin doesn't see much of a physical resemblance between him and his mother, she does. One of the first questions she asked him over the phone was whether he had blue eyes like hers. He has dark eyes. Joanne sees some of herself in his face, but mostly it's their personality and mannerisms that are strikingly similar. They both have this habit of putting their hands on top of their heads when they're thinking hard or getting ready to say something. It's uncanny.

They went back up to the room, and Joanne's sister kept calling. Finally, Kevin took the phone. "Where's my macaroni? You didn't make the meatballs yet?" he asked.

"Come over right now!"

They all trooped over to East Meadow, just ten minutes away. Joanne's sister laid on a huge spread, like my family does. She produced enough of her famed meatballs, sauce, pasta, mozzarella, prosciutto, manicotti, and cannoli to feed thirty people. Kevin was overwhelmed, and not just by the food. He met his aunts, uncles, and cousins all in one day. They had a million questions. It was a huge family reunion.

Mother and son spent the next few days together at Kevin's home in Connecticut. He wanted her to get to know his wife and kids. One day, he decided he wanted to see the Angel Guardian Home—the one place they'd been together before he was adopted. They drove to Bay Ridge, Brooklyn, and stopped outside the building. It's a grim, Dickensian-looking institution built of brown bricks—just how you'd imagine a place like that might look. The bars were still on the windows. Being there with her grown-up son was bringing back a flood of painful memories. Kevin wanted to take a look inside, but Joanne was too agitated, so he went ahead without her. Joanne stayed in the car and looked out the window. She'll never forget that moment: "Just as he bent down to look through the bars in the windows, it started to rain. Here was this man, forty-four years later, checking out the place where he'd spent his first few days of life. I had so many mixed emotions. It had been the last and only time we could be under the same roof together. Until now."

FEELING CHEATED

As happy as they are to have found each other, there's an anger and sadness that's always under the surface because they've had to miss so much of each other's lives. It's been bittersweet in the truest sense of the word.

"I lost forty-four years with him," says my aunt. "I see pictures of him at his graduation and his wedding and I think to myself, *I should have been there*. I look at pictures of my granddaughters and it kills me that I wasn't around when they were born. All those birthdays and Christmases, all those moments I couldn't be a part of . . . I look at pictures of his friends, pictures of him playing baseball, pictures of him in his football uniform—I missed that, and it breaks my heart."

More than feeling sad, though, Joanne is angry. She blames her father for ruining her chances of happiness with his hateful prejudice. And Kevin feels the same way. "I did have great parents. But do I feel cheated still? Absolutely! To some extent, I understand it as a man—times being what they were—that he figured the best thing would be to stick her with the nuns. But to cast me out of the family because I had Puerto Rican blood?"

More than anything, his heart breaks for Joanne, because she had to suffer in silence and loneliness for most of her adult life. But neither of them discusses these feelings with the other. "I don't say anything because I don't want to depress him," says Joanne.

Instead, she focuses on what she does have: a present and future with her newfound son. Over the last six years, Joanne and Kevin have grown closer and closer. After a birth parent and child first discover each other, the road isn't always so smooth. Sometimes it's too much pressure. Sometimes parent and child come from such different backgrounds that they clash. Their values aren't the same. They don't know how to fit in each other's lives. But not in this case. Joanne's relationship with her son is the best thing that happened to her. Ever since they first met, they've been catching up on a lifetime. Kevin calls Joanne "Mom." In his mind, she is his mother, just as the woman who raised him was his mother. Joanne is also

"Grandma" to his girls. They call a few times a week and see each other every one or two months—whenever they can. They celebrate holidays together. Their entire families are integrated now.

"It's been an adjustment, because all of a sudden my wife has a mother-in-law again," jokes Kevin. "I thought it was over, but Mother's Day is back."

WINNING THE LOTTO

So is Father's Day. With Joanne's help, Kevin has also reunited with his birth father. Ruben has always lived in his old neighborhood, so he wasn't difficult to find. Kevin first met him two years ago, and Ruben and his family have been another joyful addition to Kevin's life. Ruben is a good person, solid and up-standing. He's worked for PepsiCo for the past thirty years. He's a devoted family man with a wife, a daughter, and a son. Kevin is thrilled to have more siblings. He never had a sister before. And the Lopez family loves him to death. They also feel cheated out of a life with Kevin. His younger brother asked, "Where were you when I was little? I could have used a big brother when I was getting beat up in school!"

He's also part of an extended Puerto Rican clan. He calls his birth father "Dad," and Ruben's wife "Mom," just as he refers to Aunt Joanne and Joe as "Mom and Dad."

"I feel like I hit the lotto," Kevin says.

But Joanne and Kevin still make time for just the two of them. Kevin recently spent five days on his own with Joanne and Joe at her condo in Jupiter. They cooked, ate, and went food shopping together. Like most Italians, their quality time is all about food. Joanne couldn't stop feeding him! They went swimming in her pool. They fed the ducks in the backyard. They went to the beach. Joe, Joanne's husband, was also in the picture. He and Kevin are the best of friends. But Kevin's favorite part of the week was waking up early with Aunt Joanne—they're both early risers. He would put on the coffee, and then the two of them would sit out on the porch, breaking out the photo albums and trading stories.

This reunion has been healing for my entire family. Something like this—a forced adoption—ripples through and affects everyone. It matters a lot. My second cousins—the other kids in the family—are appalled by what Uncle Frankie did. They never knew. But Joanne's female first cousins were close to her, so they were always aware of the situation, and it troubled them deeply. The last thing anyone told my aunt Patty Lou before she died of ovarian cancer was that I'd found Joanne's son. She smiled, and passed away soon after.

My mother never did get a chance to meet Kevin or see Aunt Joanne reunited with her son before she died, in 2010. I'd kept my mom's confidence for six years, never disclosing to Joanne that she was the one who had revealed her secret to me. But with my mother gone, I had to let Joanne know what Mom had put me up to, and why. I wanted her to understand just how much her friendship meant to my mother, and what a precious gift she'd given her. After the funeral, I sent her an e-mail message, explaining all: "She knew you longed for him and she wanted to do this for you, so please know that it wasn't by accident. Mom didn't want you to think that she'd broken your confidence, but she also thought that you needed to know where Kevin was. So it's because of her that you now have an amazing relationship with your son."

Aunt Joanne's reply to me was short but said it all: "Thank you for letting me know that. He's my world."

The Lesson: Secrets Do Damage

Family secrets can drag you down with shame, but the truth will set you free.

It's impossible to underestimate the shame and fear that clouded adoptions for many generations. My own mother knew I'd been doing this work for more than ten years, and yet she had never so much as whispered the fact that this had been going on in our own family. Even though I openly discussed these cases with Mom, she was silent. It was shocking to me that she would take so long to spill it. And yet something inside finally drove her to tell me.

But look what happened when she finally did reveal the truth about Joanne. In the end, it was probably easier for my mom to break the silence than it would have been for Joanne, who'd been living undercover with her sadness all these decades. Many a birth mother who has finally come clean and told her family about the child she had to give up has found this to be healing. Disclosing what happened is a way of unburdening. They have to understand that women today are not viewed in the same way and that they have nothing to be ashamed of. Those were the times. If anything, these women deserve compassion for all those years of heartache and guilt they endured.

If a family walks away from you for telling them about a long-lost child, there is a dysfunction among its members that has to do with more than that particular secret. Family members should be accepting of one another no matter what the circumstances are. It's my belief that secrecy and lies are what upset people and damage relationships—not a child who comes back into the life of the birth mother.

CHAPTER SIX

A Mother's Love

• • •

Life as she knew it changed forever on the day that Johnette Crawford found out her grandmother was dying.

A southern belle from Mobile, Alabama, Johnette was born in 1968. For the first nine years of her life, she was raised by Mama Rosie, her father's mother, who also happened to be the grandmother of Melvin Franklin, the bass singer in the Temptations. Johnette worshiped her grandmother, but there was something she didn't know. She was led to believe that Rosie was her mother, and even though her father was in the picture and living under the same roof, he did nothing to disabuse her of this notion. Obviously, mother and son didn't act like man and wife, but this family structure was all Johnette had ever known, so she didn't question it. "I didn't know how it goes. All I knew was Mama," she said.

With Mama Rosie on her way out of this world, it was time for the truth to come out. Johnette's aunt Rosabelle, Melvin's mother, sat her down and told her what was really going on. Not only did she find out she was about to lose the only mother she knew to heart failure, Johnette also discovered that the life she'd been living was a lie. Johnette's real mother was in prison. Her birth mother became pregnant when she was sixteen and, about six months after Johnette was born, she left her child with Mama Rosie, her boyfriend's mother, to find work up north. She ran into some trouble while she was in New York. Allegedly, a man had tried to assault her, and she killed him in self-defense. Whatever the real story was, Johnette's birth mother was doing hard time for manslaughter.

Mama Rosie decided it would be for the best if Johnette never knew her real mother existed. She was a devout church lady and she viewed Johnette's mother as a fallen woman. Rosie meant well. She was just trying to preserve the innocence of her beloved granddaughter. She was terrified that someone would try to take Johnette away from her, or that outside influences would corrupt her.

Mama Rosie belonged to an extreme born-again Christian sect and she followed their tenets blindly. Female members of the congregation were not permitted to wear pants or short skirts. Girls had a curfew—they had to be inside their homes and off the streets long before the streetlamps came on in the evening. Johnette had to attend church at least three times a week and serve as an usher, and singing in the church choir was mandatory. She had to be in bed by 9:00 P.M., and most television shows were considered unfit for a young lady to watch. Between the church, her Catholic school, and her grandmother's strict household, Johnette's world was small and sheltered. She was beyond innocent. She was dangerously naïve.

RUDE AWAKENING

Johnette was more devastated that her grandmother lay dying than upset about the lies. But slowly she was starting to understand. It was around the same time that her real mother was released from prison. She came by Mama Rosie's house to meet her daughter for the first time. From her sickbed, Rosie introduced the stranger to Johnette as "Dorothy." The woman asked

Johnette if she could talk to her and the two went outside to sit on the porch steps.

"I am your mother," she told Johnette.

"No, you're not."

"Child, didn't anyone explain this to you? I was the one who always sent you those boxes of clothes."

Dorothy used to wire the money she earned in prison to her sister, who would send gifts and parcels on birthdays and at Christmas, but that was news to Johnette.

The arrival of her real mother into her life didn't change anything for Johnette. Dorothy was unemployed and a former felon, so she wasn't in a position to take her daughter home with her, not that Mama Rosie's family would have allowed it. Instead, when her grandmother finally passed away in 1978, Johnette was sent to live with the daughter of the church's pastor, Miss Marion. It wasn't a legal guardianship, but Mama Rosie made the request in her will. She felt that only the pastor and her family were qualified to guard Johnette's purity. She figured they'd keep her in line and continue her God-fearing upbringing.

As Johnette got older, she began to rebel. She started bonding with her birth mother and she often used to stay over at her maternal aunt's house, where Dorothy was living. Far away from the prying eyes of church ladies on the other side of town, Johnette was enjoying her newfound freedom. She got friendly with an older man—he was twenty-two at the time. At six feet two, with coffee-colored skin, reddish hair, and large green eyes, he was too handsome for the young girl to resist, and things happened. She didn't know it was forbidden, or that there would be consequences. No one told her about these things. She was only fourteen at the time.

"I knew nothing about sex. All of a sudden I was pregnant," she recalled.

WHISPERS AND LIES

She was pregnant with twins. Her guardian, Miss Marion, did her best to keep it a secret. The woman, along with her pastor mother, wouldn't allow Johnette to attend church. As heads of the congregation, they didn't want the scandal of a pregnant teenager under their roof. Johnette used to hear them discuss in whispers what was to be done with the unborn children, but never directly with her. On one occasion, she overheard Miss Marion telling the social worker they wanted her to get rid of the babies, but Johnette wasn't sure what they meant by that. The idea of giving up her babies was unthinkable. They were hers, and no one could take them away.

She continued to attend middle school. But on May 21, 1983, when she was six months pregnant and starting to show, a young boy ran into her in the hallway and landed headfirst into her belly. Johnette's water broke, and she had to be rushed to the hospital. The secret was out.

It was a tough labor, but Johnette's infant daughters—Janet and Janice—were surprisingly healthy despite such a premature birth. When she left the hospital, she took a peek in the nursery to check on her girls. Both babies were alive and well. She was told the twins would need to be kept in incubators for several weeks, until they were strong enough to go home, but she could visit them every day.

The minute she walked through the door to Miss Marion's house, the phone rang. It was the hospital. Miss Marion spoke with the hospital administrator for a while, turned to Johnette to tell her one of the babies had died, then passed the phone to her. It was Janet who had died. But what was odd was that this was less than half an hour after Johnette had seen both infants, and of the two girls, it was Janice who had the most problems. If anyone wasn't going to make it, it would have been her.

"I never believed it," said Johnette. "It was just so strange that the twins were doing so good when I was at the hospital. How could things have turned around so fast?"

Johnette asked if she could see her dead infant's body, to say good-bye, but Marion wouldn't allow it. "She said there was no need, and that it would just upset me. She refused to take me to the hospital."

For the next four months, baby Janice stayed in the hospital, and whenever Johnette could arrange for a ride from an aunt, uncle, or friend, she went to see her. She spent hours holding the surviving infant and bonding with her. One friend from church in particular was sympathetic and realized that Miss Marion and the social worker on the case were against these visits, so whenever he could, he'd sneak Johnette to the hospital in his car. "He knew all the wrong that was being done to me," she explained.

But when it was time for baby Janice to be released from the hospital, Miss Marion took over. Even though she wasn't Johnette's legal guardian and had no legal say over the fate of her child, she arranged for Janice, the surviving twin, to go into foster care. Johnette may have been sheltered most of her life, but she was bright and educated enough to know that was wrong. The social worker on her case tried to convince her to go along with it. She was told that if she insisted on keeping her baby, she would not have a home to go back to, because Miss Marion wasn't having any illegitimate children under her roof. This battle of wills went on for almost two years, but Johnette was a minor with nowhere to go. Her father, birth mother, aunts, and uncles were either unaware of what was happening or incapable of doing anything about it. It seems everyone in that tiny Southern community was under the thumb of their church, and no one was willing to stand up for the vulnerable girl and her defenseless baby, at least not until it was too late.

SEVERED TIE

Once Janice was removed from the hospital and taken into temporary care, no one would tell Johnette where her baby was. Every day, she harassed the social worker by phone so that she could be taken to see Janice. Finally, the social worker relented. "She just got so sick of me calling," Johnette explained.

She arranged for Johnette to be driven to the offices of the Department of Human Resources, so the girl could visit with Janice. By now, the baby was sixteen months old. Johnette was given less than an hour to play and cuddle with her little girl. Janice was small for her age, and there were obviously some developmental problems, but the child appeared to be healthy. Johnette wanted nothing more than to hold on to her and never let her go.

"I should have taken her and run away. I wanted to do it so bad, but when I peeped my head out of the door, I saw a lady coming down the hall and I got really scared."

One day soon after her visit, the social worker came by Miss Marion's house with a document for her to sign. She told Johnette that the papers were to give permission to temporarily house Janice with another family until Miss Marion could be convinced to let the baby come and live with Johnette at her house. But by now, Johnette was suspicious of everything these adults told her, so she read the documents carefully. "The understanding I got was that I would never see Janice again."

Miss Marion and the social worker were relentless. They kept telling her that signing the papers was in her own best interest, but Johnette wasn't buying it. She called her mother's sister, who told her not to sign anything. The social worker finally left, but the next day Johnette was summoned to court. The state was taking action to terminate her parental rights, forever.

DEEMED UNFIT

It was a kangaroo court. No one was representing Johnette's legal interests. She managed to slip out for five minutes and get to a pay phone to call her aunt, but Johnette was completely alone in this fight. Her aunt contacted Johnette's birth parents, as well as the young man who had fathered Janice, to tell them what was happening. The man's mother was more than happy to provide a home for Johnette and her grandchild, as were several aunts, uncles, and cousins on both sides of the family. Johnette's mother and father showed up in court and stated their willingness to take in their daughter and grandchild, but Johnette's birth parents weren't even considered. Her mother had a criminal record and wasn't even allowed inside the court-room. Her father had also done time on drug charges, although this was news to Johnette.

A few years later, she got hold of the court documents and saw each family member described in dehumanizing and dis-missive terms. Accounts of their state of health, their physical appearance, their relationship, and their employment histories were cold, clinical, and insulting. The fact that they were blood relatives willing to care for Janice didn't seem to have any rele-vance. Several eligible family members, including the Tempta-tion singer's mother, Aunt Rosabelle, were willing to raise the baby, but the state never notified them of the situation. The social worker even lived next door to Johnette's maternal uncle, and she spoke to him on a daily basis. Legally, she was supposed to contact all blood relatives to see if the child could be placed, but he never knew about the case. He had no idea this woman was involved in severing the birth rights of his niece.

It was as if the whole family, on both sides, had been written off as unfit to raise one of their own. Worst of all was the de-scription of Johnette. Those involved in the case implied she was an uncaring mother, stating that arrangements had been made for her to visit with the baby on several occasions but that she never showed up. Either they were lying or the arrangements had been made through Miss Marion, who was disinclined to tell Johnette about them. The court records also said that Johnette would never amount to anything, and that she would most likely abuse her child, because she came from a broken home.

"I wasn't from any broken home! My grandmother raised me and raised me good until I was ten years old! She brought me up to be a lady!" said Johnette.

With the odds stacked so high against her, Johnette lost her child. Janice was put up for adoption, and that was the beginning of a lifelong pursuit to find her. But first, Johnette was more determined than ever to make something of her life. She wanted to build up the financial independence to be a good mother and provide for her child when she eventually found her. She wanted to prove the court records wrong.

MAKING GOOD

She aced high school, graduated, and went on to college, where she studied nursing. Hardworking and blessed with a razor-sharp intellect, Johnette was able to free herself from Miss Marion's clutches by the time she was eighteen. She moved to Birmingham, Alabama, where she found a job running the office and doing the books for a local doctor. On the side, she built up a successful business doing medical billing from her home. She still runs the company alongside her husband of almost twenty years, Aundra. The only thing missing in her life was her child. Johnette wanted desperately to be a mother but, although she and her husband tried, she was never able to conceive again. It seemed as if life was playing another one of its cruel jokes on her.

When I first got the call from Johnette Crawford, I thought she was crazy. Initially, I didn't want to take her case, but Johnette was persistent. The story of how her child came to be given up for adoption just didn't seem possible in this day and age. The 1980s weren't that long ago, but this sounded like something from the turn of the last century. And yet everything she told me checked out. What happened to Johnette was a disgrace. It gave me a whole new insight into just how easily mothers and their children can lose their birthright when they're poor, underage, or undereducated. When babies have babies, they're at the mercy of church and state—of adults who say they're doing what's best for the child but are really only looking out for their own reputations.

By the time she came to me, Johnette had already done her homework. She had never stopped looking. As soon as she turned eighteen, she started making inquiries about the fate of her children. She went to the state health department to look up the death record of Janet to confirm if she really was dead. She obtained a death certificate, although a part of her still can't believe it. "After what I've been through, I don't trust the state," she told me.

She's equally unimpressed with the church. Looking back, Johnette sees it as something other than what she now believes a Christian community should represent. "A lot of girls in the church probably went through similar things. You couldn't have children out of wedlock. No way. They had an image to uphold."

Johnette focused on the daughter she knew to be alive. She went to the hospital where Janice was born and obtained copies of all her child's medical records. She petitioned and received copies of all the court records. She pestered other church members to see if they knew anything about Janice's whereabouts. If they did, no one was talking. She tracked down the foster mother who looked after Janice for the first year of her life. The lady, Miss Eunice, was kind and genuinely wanted to help. But she had been given no information. Janice had been taken from her without a word. One day out of the blue, the social worker on the case told Miss Janice to meet her in Montgomery, Alabama. The social worker took the baby into a back room, and that was the last time Miss Janice saw her. She'd always wondered what had happened to the child.

FALSE LEADS

Every so often, Johnette would get a call or a letter from one of Miss Marion's relatives. These people would say they'd seen Janice and knew where she was, but these were false leads that left Johnette a little more deflated each time. They'd give her a name and say that Janice was in the state, but this couldn't have been further from the truth. She couldn't understand why they would be so cruel, unless it was to throw her completely off the scent. They sent her on so many wild-goose chases, she stopped taking their calls. "It was their goal to never let me see Janice again," explained Johnette.

Fast-forward to 2006, when Johnette's husband, Aundra, happened to be watching DMC's documentary on VH1. When he realized what it was about, and that I could do the same thing for his wife, he taped the show and called Johnette. "When you get home, I want you to watch it. This lady may be able to find your daughter," he told her.

At first, Johnette was reluctant. She'd had her hopes raised so many times over the last twenty-two years, she didn't want to be disappointed again. She'd also thrown away thousands of dollars on those charlatans who advertise online, take your money, and come up empty. She was about to give up the search altogether. About a month later, she watched the show, but she still wasn't convinced. "Yeah, yeah. It ain't for me. She ain't gonna find her," she said.

But that Christmas, she had a change of heart. She'd give it one last shot. Her New Year's resolution for 2007 was to put everything she could into one last big search. She sent me an e-mail, then another, then another. As I said, the story sounded too crazy to be a legitimate case. But Johnette's determination was impressive. I finally wrote her back and asked her to send me all the information she had. I didn't hear from her again. I assumed my first instincts were right. I wrote her off as a nut job.

Johnette had typed up everything and sent it, but she must have sent it to the wrong e-mail address, or maybe it landed in my spam file. She wrote me off, too, as "another one of those scams," in her words.

January and February passed. Johnette and Aundra had gone back to Mobile for the Mardi Gras. The memories came flooding back. Knowing it was on her mind, Aundra asked Johnette if she'd heard from me, and when she told him no, he insisted she call me to make sure I had received all the material. When we finally spoke, we cleared up the misunderstanding and Johnette e-mailed me the information again. There was plenty to go on. Birth mothers usually have more information than adoptees, although that depends on the truthfulness of the official documents. In this case, I kept hitting dead ends. But after running tons of data, I found a lead.

LAST KNOWN ADDRESS

By the next day, I knew which family had taken Janice, and why it had been so hard to find her. Janice was born Janice La-Shay Crawford, but her middle and last names had been changed. The family had moved around a lot. The adoptive father was in the military, and within a few years of Janice's adoption, they had moved to a base in Germany. Since Janice was a military brat, there was no way Johnette could have tracked her down.

But I managed to connect the dots and found an address, at least for the adoptive parents. I called them, told them I was doing some research, and learned that Janice knew she'd been adopted, and that she'd moved out of the house when she was eighteen. The last they knew of her, she was working at an Arby's. I had a location and some names, and a last known address for Janice. I couldn't pinpoint her exact location. As far as I could tell, she was moving every few weeks. But we were close enough, so I gave Johnette a call.

"Hey Johnette, name some of the major towns in your state." She went through the list until she finally hit the right place. "That's it!"

"Huh? You want me to find an address for you?"

"No, silly! I want you to get ready for a road trip. That's where your daughter lives."

Johnette had no idea why I was asking about these towns. It didn't occur to her that I could have already located her daughter. For the past several years, she'd been living only forty-five minutes away.

It was Friday night at nine and Johnette was ready to leave that minute. But Aundra told her to stay put. If they'd left then, they wouldn't have arrived until about 10:00 P.M.—not a wise hour to be knocking on doors. The last thing he wanted was to raise suspicions and kill their chances of ever finding Janice.

That night, Johnette didn't sleep. She got up at dawn and grabbed the only baby picture of Janice she'd cajoled out of the social worker when she saw her child for the final time. She put on her sneakers, hat, and coat, ready to hit the road. She stood over her bleary-eyed husband until he was ready, too. They didn't even stop for coffee. "Let's go," she told Aundra. "My baby is waiting for us."

They were at Janice's last known address by 6:00 A.M. The windows were dark and the place still had Christmas lights hanging around the door. Johnette rang the bell, but no one answered. She asked a girl who was coming out of the building if she knew Janice.

"She don't live here no more," she said. "Who are you?"

"I'm looking for Janice. I am her birth mother."

"For real? Go across the hall. The guy living there knows her. His name is T. His wife went to school with her."

Johnette knocked on T.'s door and he opened it, rubbing his eyes and yawning. Johnette and Aundra were a well-dressed, respectable-looking, middle-class, middle-aged black couple who drove a silver Jaguar. It was clear this wasn't their neighborhood, but they were in no way threatening.

"Can I help you?" T. finally asked.

"I need to speak with you about Janice."

"What's wrong with Janice?"

She told him her story and showed him the picture.

"Man! Come on in! Janice is going to be so happy!" he said.

"She knows she's adopted?"

"Are you kidding me? She's been looking for you! She don't know who you are, but ever since I met Janice all she's been sayin' is, 'I'm gonna find my mama.'"

T. gave them a hug and they all started crying. He took their information and promised to get his wife to call when she got home from work that afternoon. Johnette and Aundra were about to leave and book a room at a hotel, when they saw some other girls coming out of the apartment. T. pointed out one of the women and suggested they ask her if she knew anything. She'd also been friends with Janice. The girls were excited and escorted the couple to all the other rooming houses where Janice used to live. Then they took Johnette and Aundra to Janice's last known place of work, a Hardees restaurant. They asked to speak to a manager, who was reluctant to talk to them, but a young woman, an assistant manager, took Johnette aside. "I understand exactly how you feel," she said. "Wait right here."

The woman pulled out Janice's old job application, which

contained several addresses and phone numbers, as well as contacts for personal references. They went through all the numbers, calling them on Johnette's cell phone. Each time, either the number had been disconnected or Janice had just moved—a month ago, two weeks ago, a week ago. They kept missing her. Janice was moving from one rooming house to another, and from one job to another. She was basically homeless.

It was looking hopeless, but when they got down to the last number, which was for a guy we'll call David, a woman answered the phone. Her name was Miss Dorothy, another name that was listed as a reference on the job application.

"Hi, ma'am, I'm looking for David. Is he at home?"

"What's wrong with David? That's my son!"

Johnette told her the whole story, saying that she was Janice's birth mother and that she'd been looking for her daughter these past twenty-two years.

"Why didn't you say so! Where are you now? I'll come right over!" Miss Dorothy said.

Miss Dorothy and her husband pulled up ten minutes later. She got out of the car and gave Johnette and Aundra a huge hug and a kiss. "Oh Lord, oh Jesus, thank you!" she exclaimed. I've been praying for this day ever since I met that poor child. Janice needs her mother. And she looks just like you, too!"

"Have you seen her?"

"Yeah, she's working at another fast-food joint. Follow me in my car and I'll take you there."

THE RESCUE

They pulled up at a burger place on the other side of town. Miss Dorothy and her husband offered to go in first, to prepare Janice for her visitor. It was chilly outside, so Johnette and Aundra stepped into the entranceway. Janice turned around to look at her and Johnette nearly passed out from the shock. It was the first time she'd seen her daughter since she was a baby, but she would have known her straightaway. They had the same face. But what was disturbing was Janice's general demeanor.

"She had nappy hair and she was going bald on one side of her head. Her skin was ashy, she was skin and bones, and she was all dingy and dirty. She had a look in her eyes, she was twitchy, and for a minute I thought maybe she was on crack," Johnette recalled.

There were no drugs involved, just years of suffering. Janice couldn't even look people in the eye. She was like a broken bird just waiting for her mother to come and fix her. But at first, she didn't believe her life was about to change.

Johnette introduced herself. "Hi, Janice, my name is Johnette Crawford."

"So what?"

"I am your mother."

"Huh?"

"I am your birth mother. I have been looking for you for twenty-two years."

"You are not my mother! Stop playing with me! I am tired of people playing with me!"

Johnette showed the girl her baby picture. That did it. Janice started screeching. "Mama, Mama, Mama! Where were you? I been looking all over for you, too. I just didn't know how!"

By now, everyone was crying. Johnette told her daughter to ask the restaurant manager if she could go on break for an hour, or take the rest of the day off, so they could get to know each other and decide what they were going to do next. But the woman in charge wasn't having it. Coincidentally, Janice had just told everyone the day before that she was adopted. Her boss thought the whole thing was a trick so Janice could get out of work. Johnette showed the woman her baby picture, but she just folded her arms, shook her head, said, "No, Janice cannot leave."

"But after all we showed you, you won't let her take even a few minutes off?" Johnette asked.

"No way!"

Aundra stepped in. "Ma'am, this is serious. You mean to tell me you are not going to let my wife talk to her daughter?"

"Hell no!"

"Janice, how much do you make at this place?" Aundra asked.

The store manager told them it was none of their business, but Janice spoke up. She made seven dollars an hour. The wages were so low, she could barely afford to clothe and feed herself.

"Janice, do you want to go with me, your mother? It's gonna be a rough road ahead. We have a lot of catching up to do, and there's a lot I'll have to teach you. But we'll work through it."

"I want to go with you, Mama. There's nothing for me here."

"Well, all right, then."

Johnette took charge. It was time to be a mom, and it gave her great pleasure to politely tell Janice's unreasonable boss to go to hell.

"Ma'am, I am sorry to inform you that this will be Janice's last day of employment here. Janice, you go ahead and clock out, hang up your hat, and come on home with me."

Janice was like an excited little kid. She took off her uniform and told all the other waitresses what had just transpired. "I'm going home with my mama. My real mama! She's come to get me!"

Their first stop was Taco Bell, where they had lunch. Janice ate like a starving animal. She ordered six tacos and gobbled them down one by one. Then they stopped by the rooming house where Janice was staying, and she went in to gather all her belongings. When Janice came out, it nearly broke Johnette's heart. All she had was a Walmart bag with a pair of dirty sneakers, some toothpaste, and a toothbrush. All she owned were the shabby clothes on her back.

Their next stop was the home of Janice's pastor, one of the

few people who seemed to care about the girl. There were more hugs all around, and then he prayed for them.

Their last stop was the home of her adoptive parents. Janice called ahead and said, "I got a surprise for you."

CLEAN BREAK

When the Crawfords showed up at the door with Janice, only the adoptive mother was at home. The woman was stone cold and silent. It was a strange reaction. A normal response to the sight of your daughter at the door, accompanied by a grown man and woman, would be to ask, "Who is this?" But the woman said nothing. She walked to the back of the living room and stood by the fireplace, just staring. At one point, she went off to another room and they heard whispers, but they didn't know to whom she was speaking. Maybe she was praying. When she came out again after fifteen minutes, she sat down and took a deep breath. Finally, Johnette told her who she was.

"I am Janice's mother."

"I knew you were going to find your baby," the woman said.

She started sobbing, and Johnette went over to hug her. "It's okay," said Johnette, consoling her. "Sometimes life takes you through these things."

Looking back, Johnette realized these were probably tears of remorse. The woman called her husband to tell him what was happening, but he was at work and couldn't get away. At no point did she try to convince Janice to stay.

Johnette has a hunch the couple had a connection with the church back in Mobile. It was entirely possible that they knew Miss Marion and were aware of the circumstances that had resulted in Janice's being taken away from her real mother. She couldn't prove it, but the woman had a way of looking at her that made her suspect this. "She just stared dead at me, like she knew something I didn't," Johnette recalled.

There was a lot about the way Janice had been raised that Johnette didn't know, either. It would all come out as mother and daughter got acquainted over the next few days. Johnette wasn't surprised to learn that the girl's adoptive mother had no maternal feelings for her. She had seen that for herself. Instead, Janice was regarded as more of a nuisance at home, and her presence was deeply resented. Janice's adoptive mother had beaten her regularly.

"I got whooped and backhanded for every little thing," said Janice, whose adoptive mother even tried to choke her on one occasion.

Janice was developmentally challenged because of her premature birth. There were problems that could have been corrected with a little extra attention, or at least with the normal amount of parental love and guidance, but her issues got worse due to total neglect. The school system gave up on her and passed her through each grade without even trying to teach her the basics. She couldn't count. They had put her on Ritalin to keep her under control, and Janice sleepwalked her way through life. If she had a question for her adoptive mother, she was told to stop being a pest and was sent to her room.

The extended family always treated her like an outsider. At family barbecues and holiday dinners, no one talked to her, not even the grandmother. The only attention she got was the wrong kind. When she was six years old, her older cousin, a grown woman, sexually abused her. Janice told no one in her family because she knew they wouldn't believe her and it would result in another beating.

Of the entire clan, only her adoptive father was kind to her. It had been his idea to adopt. He was basically a decent man. His brother had adopted some children, and it seemed like the right thing to do at the time. The adoptive mother hadn't been so sure. She'd never wanted kids. There were no other children in the family.

Janice's parents never directly admitted she was adopted. But as long as she could remember, Janice had felt something was wrong. "I never felt like I fit in," she explained.

She learned the truth when she was eleven. While she was home alone, she went through some papers in the file cabinet and came across her birth records and adoption papers. The documents said she had a twin sister who had died. When she confronted her parents about this a few days later, they told her they didn't know what she was talking about. The truth was already out there, but they refused to acknowledge it.

But Janice never forgot. She used to go to Walmart and wander down the aisles, looking at older women and wondering, *Is she my mother?* She called an agency to see if they could find her birth mother, but she was told she was too young, and that it would cost her money she didn't have.

Janice started working as soon as she turned sixteen. It was her goal to get out of the house as soon as she could save enough money. Her adoptive parents wouldn't even allow her to drive, and she didn't get her license until she was nineteen, a year after she moved out. For five years, she worked long hours for Taco Bell, a job her adoptive father had helped her get. But she was barely subsisting. Her adoptive mother had set up a bank account for Janice, and added her own name to the account. Knowing her daughter had never learned how to count, she had been helping herself to large chunks of Janice's paycheck ever since. Janice had a 401(K), but somehow she could never get access to her own money. When Johnette looked into the situation and called the bank, she discovered that the adoptive mother had changed the PIN code and had been dipping into Janice's pension plan account, as well.

BROKEN BIRD

The more Janice got comfortable with Johnette and Aundra in her new home, the more she opened up about what her life had been like. It was as if she'd been raised by wolves.

"She was just so broken. Like a little stray puppy with no one around to look after her," Johnette recalled.

Janice didn't even own a bra. Instead, she supported her breasts by wrapping an old T-shirt around her chest and tying a knot in the middle. She had no grounding in the basics of womanhood, things that we all take for granted. She had no mother to guide her, and she'd long since fallen through the cracks of the education system. Johnette had to teach her everything from scratch.

The new family had T-shirts made to commemorate the day Johnette found Janice—March 3, 2007—the beginning of the rest of their lives together. Within a month of moving in with Johnette, Janice decided she might as well make the relationship official. She insisted that her mother take her downtown to the local Bureau of Vital Statistics so she could legally change her name back to the original: Janice LaShay Crawford. Janice didn't stop there. She had her mother's name tattooed on her arm.

But their first year as mother and daughter was a roller-coaster ride. Janice and Aundra became instant buddies. Johnette's husband is a teddy bear, and he had always been supportive of her quest to find Janice. But Janice was resistant to Johnette's rules. She'd been allowed to run wild for so long that the structure of her new life took some getting used to. "We had a lot of bumps and bruises that first year," recalled Johnette. "There was a lot of stuff to straighten out."

Johnette took on the role of teacher. She discovered that although Janice was a little slow to comprehend, her level of intelligence was normal. Johnette took her daughter to the Alabama

Department of Rehabilitation Services and signed her up with a social worker, who did an evaluation and confirmed that there was nothing mentally wrong with Janice. If anything, she was a naturally bright girl. She'd been written off as mildly retarded and kept in a state of ignorance for the convenience of people who either wanted to keep her under control or who simply couldn't be bothered with the child. But when someone took the time to patiently explain and repeat things, Janice could learn and remember anything.

Johnette enrolled her in a local cosmetology school, and each year Janice made the dean's list. After two years, she graduated with top marks. (Her adoptive parents showed up at the graduation, although they didn't stick around for dinner.) Meanwhile, Johnette filled in the gaps. She went to a teacher's store and bought her daughter a tray of fake money to teach her how to count. She played counting games with Janice over and over again until she could do the math in her head as quickly as anyone. She helped her set up her own bank account and explained to her how to write checks. She taught her how to keep track of her expenses and set aside money for savings. She also had to teach Janice how to put herself first and not be so trusting. The girl had a dangerous habit of giving her money and her heart away to anyone who ever said a kind word to her. Since her early teens, she'd been in a string of abusive relationships, including the one with her last boyfriend.

"I had to teach her everything I knew," Johnette said. "In case something happened to me, I wanted her to be able to stand on her own two feet."

FROM SCRATCH

Johnette also had to teach her daughter social skills. She could be so painfully shy that she spoke with her head down and wouldn't look people in the eye. Other times, she had no filter, and she would blurt out the first thing that came into her mind. At times, she could easily have been mistaken for someone who had Asperger's syndrome, but the truth was that she'd had no adults in her life whose appropriate behavior she could emulate. No one had taught her how to act.

"It was like taking a grown woman back to being a child," Johnette explained.

Janice got frustrated. She'd been left on her own for so long that there were times she resented having to answer to her mother. On one occasion, Johnette was trying to teach her daughter something, and Janice got so angry that she walked out of the house still dressed in her pajamas. Johnette searched the streets for her for hours. She finally tracked her down at the home of one of Janice's cosmetology school friends, Tiffany. It was the one day Tiffany didn't call Janice, which made Johnette suspicious. When she knocked on the door, Tiffany was startled to see her. Johnette put her hand to Tiffany's mouth and warned her to keep quiet. Then she found a belt.

"You better not tell her I'm here, or I'll pop you one, too. Now where is she?" Johnette said to Tiffany.

Johnette was led to a room where Janice lay sleeping, and she flicked on the light. When Janice lifted her head off the pillow, startled, Johnette grabbed her by the shirt and gave her a whooping she never forgot. "I beat her like a little kid. I was so hurt that she would run away from me, and I was mad as hell," Johnette recalled.

The incident scared Johnette so much, she called the adoptive family to see if they would take Janice back. She didn't want her daughter running wild on the streets of Birmingham. She couldn't bear the thought of something bad happening to Janice on her watch. But when she called, they made it clear they didn't want Janice back. They told Johnette she was the only one who knew how to handle Janice, so she might as well keep her.

"Do you hear that, Janice? That means I am your mother and you are going to do what I tell you to do," Johnette said.

Things got better and better. When you see pictures of the girl Johnette first met and the young woman she's become, Janice looks like a different person. She's well groomed, dresses like a lady, and is polite and respectful—a real Southern belle, like her mom. She's developed a healthy curiosity about the world, and today she soaks up knowledge like a sponge. She keeps surprising Johnette with all the interesting facts she picks up on the History Channel. Ever the hard worker, she soon found a job at Walmart, and picked up some part-time work as a hairdresser. She found an apartment nearby, although she went home for dinner with Aundra and Johnette—whom she now calls "Mama and Daddy"—several times a week.

The family has never been closer. They are spreading their message of hope as they travel the state, giving talks to young mothers faced with similar challenges. They volunteer at a drug program, sharing their story and offering words of encouragement to women in rehab who have lost custody of their children for various reasons. They also speak to older women who were forced to give their children up for adoption.

"We let them know that anything is possible if you try and pray hard enough. They can have a happy reunion, too," Johnette said.

MENDED HEART

It didn't seem possible that Janice could love her birth mother any more than she already did, but on December 15, 2009, at the age of just forty-one, Johnette had a heart attack. The next day, she had a single bypass, but the following February, she had chest pains again. She went to the hospital for another open-heart surgery, to replace the artery, and they discovered two more arteries that were blocked. In March, she had a triple by-pass. Postsurgery, she developed pneumonia and a blood clot in her leg. In July, she had another surgery, this time to remove some fluid from her lungs. Janice almost lost the mother she'd waited her whole life to meet. She was scared. But Johnette had too many reasons to live.

"I told her I'm not going anywhere," Johnette recalled. "I'm a living testimony. Now I'm running around like a little chicken."

Janice and Aundra nursed Johnette back to health. On so many levels, Johnette's heart has healed. The two women have become each other's saviors. Just as Johnette became Janice's lifeline, Janice has become her rock. Johnette found Janice a full-time job running the reception desk of the medical prac-tice that she manages. Knowing that the day-to-day operations of her office are in Janice's safe and reliable hands has taken away some of the stress of the job, which led in part to Johnette's heart attack.

ANOTHER CHANCE

Janice has given her mother another gift. On January 4, 2011, Johnette became a grandmother. Katelyn Rose Crawford came kicking and screaming into the world at six pounds, fourteen ounces. Far from being a preemie birth like Janice was, Katelyn was born three days past the due date. When she found out she was pregnant, Janice moved back home to be closer to her mother, who is going to help her raise the child. The father of the child, Janice's boyfriend, is in the picture, but they have no immediate plans to get married. It's Johnette's opportunity to make up for lost time and help bring up the baby with the baby girl she never got to raise herself.

"Now the circle is complete. Who says you don't get second chances in life?" said Johnette.

Janice's adoptive parents showed little interest in these milestones in the years after she left home. Phone calls were rare. They almost never checked in. But when it became clear that Janice was making progress and doing well, some uncles, aunts, and cousins did start to call. One uncle invited her on a family trip up-country, but it was so out of the blue that Johnette was suspicious of his motives and advised Janice not to go. It seemed odd that relatives who showed no interest in the girl when she was in such dire straits should suddenly be so curious about her welfare. Johnette figures it might have something to do with a fear that Janice will reveal some of their dark family secrets. "They still think she's this slow child, and they probably want to coach her not to talk."

But Janice knows better, and she has plenty to say about the relatives who treated her like dirt. "I never really knew what real love from a family was supposed to be like until my real parents found me."

Both women share bitter memories of past betrayals from the very people who were supposed to care for and protect them. But their happiness in finding each other has helped them heal and let go of the past. For Johnette, the anger and resentment ran deep, but the miracle of finding Janice has restored her faith. "For a long time, I had thoughts of killing everyone that had anything to do with Janice being taken from me. But I have forgiven all of those people because every tear I cried God has wiped away by giving me back my baby."

The Lesson: A Mother's Love Is Timeless

There is an unspoken connection between a child and a mother that I see over and over again. I don't know if it's instinct or if there is a tie that goes beyond the physical, but it's undeniable. Clients often say to me, "I hope you can find my birth mother, but I feel like she's dead," or "I feel like my child is in trouble." There is some kind of telepathic connection that never ceases to amaze me.

Maybe we are never that far apart from one another. Maybe a piece of our birth family lives within us. There is something visceral about this bond. In the case of Janice and Johnette, mother and daughter saved each other. Janice needed to be saved, but in saving her, Johnette saved herself.

It's not uncommon for a birth mother to be coerced into giving up her child, for whatever reason. Most are young, naïve, and vulnerable women. I guess the other lesson here is Janice's and Johnette's capacity to forgive. They found the strength in each other to move forward. They chose not to linger on the bitterness and regret, focusing instead on the sheer joy of finally having each other in their lives.

CHAPTER SEVEN

A Father's Love

• • •

Like clockwork, Carl would get up at 6:00 A.M. every Saturday and Sunday to search the Internet. While his family still lay sleeping, he had about three to four hours alone to surf every adoption search Web site and scan every Google link that was associated with the name that might have been on his daughter's birth certificate. His wife always knew, but his two sons had no idea that their father had been haunted by this secret for forty years. They were unaware that Carl had fathered a child when he was no more than a child himself, and that she was given up for adoption against his will. They were clueless about the fact that Carl had been desperately searching for their elder sister ever since.

Each time, those searches ended in failure and disappointment. As a father, he was at an added disadvantage, because he wasn't privy to the exact name on his daughter's birth certificate, his own name wasn't anywhere on the records, and he couldn't even be sure of the exact day she was born.

"That was the way it was back then," he explained. "As far as the adoption courts were concerned, the father was just some anonymous bad guy. I was just some anonymous bad guy looking to do the right thing."

Carl was bringing me up to speed on the last four decades of his life. He found me in November 2009, when, during one of his early-morning computer vigils, he'd stumbled on the Web link of Sylvia Ackerson. She, too, was obsessed with finding her birth son, and she'd started an online support group—a Web page on the New York Adoption site—for other birth parents who were looking. When Carl contacted her and told her his story, she immediately put him in contact with me. "If anyone can find your daughter, Pam can," she said. "Just be warned. She's expensive."

I have to admit, when I got his call, I was surprised. It's rare enough for birth mothers to search, but I almost never hear from birth fathers. In all my years as a searcher, less than a handful of dads have come to me, and even fewer have been as relentless and determined as this guy. Then again, Carl is an exceptional man.

One of the first things he asked me was my fee. I told him what I tell everyone. My fee ranges from $2,000 and $2,500, depending on how much legwork is involved, but no find, no fee.

Carl laughed. "Only twenty-five hundred dollars to part the Red Sea? That's a bargain!"

I liked him immediately. We talked for what must have been more than an hour. I had to know why he was so obsessed. As an adoptee myself, I'm always fascinated to learn what's going on in the mind of the birth parent. And I need to know that they have all the right intentions.

"So why, Carl? Why is this so important to you? In all my years of doing this, I've never heard of a birth father investing this much time and effort in a search."

He let out a deep sigh. He was a natural talker, but this subject didn't come naturally to him, as he'd kept it locked away for so long.

"You know, after carrying this inside me for all these years, it feels weird to tell my story out loud, but here goes," he said.

Carl's family were fresh-off-the-boat immigrants. His father was from Croatia and his mother was from Italy. They met late in life, and had Carl when they were already in their late forties. When his parents got to the United States, there were no cousins, no aunts, no uncles, no grandparents. They left their relatives behind and never looked back. That's how it was back then. When their generation left the mother country, it was a clean break.

"I've often asked myself why I have obsessed about finding my daughter for so long. I guess it's because I come from a family that never had any family," he told me.

RUNNING WILD

It was some family. Carl's father was a merchant seaman, and he would leave his wife and child for months at a time. When he was home, he drank hard, and he wasn't a happy drunk. He was abusive, physically and verbally. But apart from his few appearances in their lives, Carl and his mother were pretty much on their own. They lived in a tiny one-bedroom apartment in Jackson Heights, Queens. Carl slept on a Castro Convertible—a lumpy old sofa bed—in the middle of the living room. His father blew his paychecks on God knows what, so Carl's mom was forced to work long hours out by the airport, at the Federal Aviation Agency, and Carl was left by himself most of the day. He was a typical latchkey kid, roaming the streets of Queens unsupervised in the late 1960s. It was a recipe for disaster.

That's when Carl hooked up with his childhood sweetheart. We'll call her Linda. Linda was also a latchkey kid. Her father had left years before and her mother worked sixty hours a week as a waitress, so Linda was left to fend for herself. She had a younger brother, who, oddly enough, I used to date in my rebellious teen years, long before Carl reached out to me. I remember that family well. They always seemed to have a hard-luck story. When I found out years later what had happened to them, I was shocked. But back when Carl and Linda were a pair of cute fifteen-year-old kids, the world seemed full of promise.

"It was the two of us against the world," recalled Carl. "We were inseparable. We were free to do whatever we wanted. What was going to happen?"

UNHEEDED WARNING

It started out innocently enough. Carl and Linda were best friends. They never argued. They looked out for each other. But as time wore on, people grew concerned. Carl's friends didn't like the relationship. "It's just you two all the time," they said. They were both sixteen when Carl's mother noticed Carl was spending too much time alone at the girl's apartment. She went to see Linda's mother and told her she thought it best if Carl no longer be allowed to stay there. Instead, she suggested they hang out together at her place, when she was home from work, so they could be supervised. Carl's mother feared the inevitable. But Linda's mom dismissed her concerns, insisting her daughter was a "good girl" and that nothing could happen.

Then one day, out of the blue, Linda came to Carl, looking serious. "Carl, listen to me," she said. "I have to go away for a while."

"Where? Where are you going? I'll come and visit."

Carl assumed that "a while" would be about a week. They'd spent every minute of every day together for the last year and a half. The idea of not seeing her was unthinkable.

"No, no! You can't come," Linda said. "You have to promise

me that you won't come and you won't try to contact me. Don't go looking for my brother, or my mom, or me. I swear I will get in touch with you, but it won't be for a long time. It could be months. But please don't come looking for me."

Carl was depressed. The months went by, and he was beginning to lose hope he'd ever hear from Linda again. He became listless. He was hardly ever in class, his grades suffered, and he was on his way to becoming a high school dropout. Then one day, about nine months later, in late October 1968, the phone in his apartment started to ring. First, his father, who was home on leave, picked it up, and there was dead silence on the other end. "Who is this? Why are you calling our house?" he screamed into the phone.

After several more tries, Carl managed to pick up before his father did, and when Linda recognized his voice, she finally spoke up.

"It's me," she said.

"What's going on?"

"We can get together now. I will meet you somewhere in the neighborhood. But don't try to find me."

They met at one of their old haunts—a small park where they weren't likely to run into anybody they knew. She told him she'd been staying with a relative of her mother's in Staten Island. She'd given birth to a baby girl.

"Of course I knew it was mine. It was only ever us. But remember, we were two kids," Carl said. "There was no sex education to speak of. We didn't know anything. So *shock* was the word for what I was feeling. I don't think it was possible for me to fully process what she was telling me at the time."

Immediately, Carl wanted to know where the baby was. He may have been a kid, but his first instinct was to take responsibility. It was his daughter, after all.

Linda said, "Don't worry about where she is. It's all over

with. My mother gave her up for adoption through the courts. Your name is nowhere on the birth record."

NO SAY

Carl's head was spinning. He certainly wasn't thinking to himself that he'd dodged a bullet. But the situation was too unreal for him to be angry. He couldn't feel outraged that she'd completely usurped his rights as a father. He didn't know what to feel. Neither of them was a minor at the time. They were both over sixteen and, legally, would have been required to sign documents saying they were giving up the child. But instead, Linda's mother took it upon herself to lie to the court, tell the judge that her daughter was fifteen, and pretend that she was the legal guardian of the baby. Apparently, it occurred to no one in the court system to ask to meet the girl or to verify that any of these statements were true. But at the time, Carl had no say in the matter. "I knew I had nothing. I had no car, no TV, no money, no place to live," he told me.

"What are we going to do?" he asked Linda.

"I don't know, but the baby is gone."

"Did you see her?"

"Yes, I saw her. She was beautiful."

"You know, we've got to try to get that baby back."

She didn't seem very enthusiastic. But Carl meant it. He'd just turned seventeen by then, and the New York Police Department was hiring recruits at the time. They wanted to suck in the best and the brightest, and Carl had just aced all the entrance exams. He was waiting for an offer, and if it came through, he could earn enough to support the three of them. It sure beat what he was doing at the time—bagging groceries at the local A&P.

NEVER THE SAME

Carl and Linda continued dating for another year. They kept talking about what they were going to do. But as the months went by, the birth of the baby seemed more and more surreal.

"To be honest, I don't think either one of us could fully process it. We knew something huge had happened, and it was ours. And I just kept thinking there had to be a way we could rectify this," he told me.

Then, almost a year to the day that Carl's daughter was born, Linda disappeared without a word. The whole family had packed up and moved away without so much as leaving a forwarding address. Carl went into another spiral. He loved his childhood sweetheart more than anything, and he was heartbroken. At six feet tall, Carl's a big brawny guy, and back in the day he lifted weights. But within six months, he'd dropped from 205 pounds to 165 pounds. He couldn't eat. That's how devastated he was. He kept looking for her, figuring there must be some logical explanation. One day, he was out with five of his friends, waiting for the number 266 bus from Flushing to Jackson Heights. One of his friends suddenly looked stricken.

"Um, Carl," he said. "Don't look now, but I think I just saw Linda, and she's with another guy."

Carl swung around, and there she was. She didn't notice him, but he saw all he needed to see. There she was, the mother of his child, walking arm and arm with another guy down the main street of Flushing.

"I was stunned. Who was this guy who was so much better than me? How could she do this? Then she walked off in the distance and I never saw her again," he told me.

Eventually, Carl made a decision to move on with his life. He'd drifted without purpose for a few months, then decided to go to college. He was determined to get a Ph.D. He'd never finished high school, and when he asked to go back to complete his senior year, the school refused to take him. Carl was seen as a troublemaker, and he had a history of getting into fights. Undaunted, he persuaded his mother to scrape together enough money to send him to a private prep school in Manhattan. It was the only way he could get his GED, and she saw the determination in his eyes when he told her he planned to do something with his life. He made good on his promise. Carl got into Queensborough, one of the free community colleges that were part of a new citywide college system for underprivileged kids. Within a year, he earned an associate's degree, then a B.A. in English literature, and, in short order, a Master's and Ph.D. in anthropology at Stony Brook University. He eventually became a successful wine dealer, married, and had two sons. He raised his family in a comfortable middle-class home on Long Island and lived a good life. But he never forgot.

WANING HOPE

While he was pursuing his studies, money was tight, but Carl kept revisiting the possibility of finding his daughter. At twenty-four, when a part-time job put a little more cash in his pocket, he called a private detective agency and told them his story. The guy who answered wasn't very encouraging, but he was honest. "It'll cost you six hundred dollars up front just to start the search, and then what? What do you expect us to do for you?" the man said.

"It's okay. I'll pay it. Whatever it takes."

"Sorry, buddy. Your name is nowhere on the birth certificate. And even if we can perform a magic trick, there are confidentiality laws. There's nothing we can do for you but take your money, and that just wouldn't be right."

He tried again in 1979. Carl had just completed his Ph.D., but there was too much missing from his life for him to celebrate this crowning achievement. This time, the investigator said it would cost one thousand dollars up front, but he warned Carl that taking the case would be like stealing his money, it was so hopeless.

Still, Carl wouldn't give up. He set about trying to find his old girlfriend and her brother. He scanned the phone book for clues. Nothing. He became an early user of the Internet, long before it was widely available. He did searches on a program called Prodigy, way before Google ever existed. He was sure it was the tool that was going to help him find his daughter. But the more time passed, the harder it was. By now, Linda had probably married and changed her name. He found out years later that she'd even used a different name on the birth certificate—her mother's alias—but fortunately he'd already guessed as much. When adoption Web pages first started to appear, he was posting both names.

By the time Carl called me, he was pretty skeptical about whether I could help him. He was sure nothing would come of it. Despite all his research skills, he was coming up empty, so he figured only a miracle worker could help him. Trust was another issue. He was using an alias himself, and a bogus e-mail address. I could understand why. People in his situation are often cagey by reflex. He had kept the secret a long time, and he was paranoid about anyone finding out before he was ready, especially his two sons. But the situation was frustrating. Not only did he have to trust me if I was going to do a delicate search like this for him; I had to be able to trust him, as well. I always need to make sure that the people who are doing the searching aren't wackos. The last thing I want is to victimize the people I find on my clients' behalf.

"Carl, come on. Enough already! You gotta get real with me, or you can forget about it," I said.

"You're right, Pam, I'm sorry. It's just hard to let go of the secrecy, you know?"

BREAKTHROUGH

I had good news for Carl, but I wanted to make sure he deserved to hear it. I'd done a very specialized kind of search, one that's tedious and intensive but almost never fails if I have the right name. I'd checked all the birth-record indexes in New York City—a territory I knew pretty well by this point—and run the names.

Carl had already done a search and confirmed his daughter's exact date of birth. Then I'd verified her information at birth and cross-referenced it with all the girls born with that name, or one of the two names she could be listed under. These were public records, and the names were in alphabetical order, so the information had been there all along. You just had to know where and how to look.

There was still a lot of verification and clarification to be done. I'm especially adept at tracking people down, but I never want to take away from that first contact for my clients, so I am careful not to tip off the people I am researching. Plus, once you've located the object of the search, you have to make damn sure they're okay with being found.

I called Carl to let him know the good news. It was that dead zone between Christmas and New Year's, and Carl happened to be at the Prospect Park Zoo, alone in the cold and staring at the sea lions, when his BlackBerry rang.

"Merry Christmas, Carl. It's me, Pam! I found her, but I need to know what you want me to do if she doesn't know she's adopted. We have to be careful before we rock this woman's world."

It's not common, but throughout my career I have come across adoptees who were unaware they had been adopted. That's why, when I reach out to an adoptee, I am extremely cautious in my approach. Carl understood my point.

"Oh God. I hadn't even thought of that. If she doesn't know, walk away," he said.

132 · PAMELA SLATON

I called his daughter and explained that I was helping someone who was looking for his biological daughter, then asked her if it was possible she was an adoptee.

"Yes, I am! Why do you ask?" she replied.

"Well, someone is looking for you. In fact, he's been looking for you your whole life. He's your birth father, and his story checks out. He's a good guy and he really wants to meet you."

It was amazing how little she knew about herself. Let's call her Krystal. Krystal didn't even know the name her mother had used on the birth certificate, alias or otherwise. All she knew was her date of birth and that her birth parents were of Italian extraction. Coincidentally, she had been raised by a big Italian-American family on Long Island, not twenty minutes from where Carl was living. She knew she was adopted, but this was a tight-knit, protective clan. In fact, Krystal had been raised well in a loving environment. Her adoptive dad was a fireman and her mom was a homemaker. She'd often wondered about where she came from and who her birth parents were, and she checked the adoption Web sites from time to time, but she felt no strong pull to do anything more about finding them—at least not at that point in her existence. She had a full life, and she had already given birth to two daughters of her own.

REALITY CHECK

It was sobering for Carl to realize that all those years he'd felt the need to connect with her, she'd had no burning need to connect with him. "I'm beginning to realize that, for all practical purposes, I am nobody in her life," he told me.

Still, finding her was a gift of closure for Carl. "Even if she never wants to meet me, I'll go to my grave knowing I did everything I could to find her, and I did find her. I'll never look back and regret not trying."

But the situation wasn't hopeless. The person who is searching has to remember to tread carefully and not push themselves too hard into the life of the person they have been searching for. Carl just had to be patient. Albeit reluctantly, Krystal allowed me to pass on her e-mail address to Carl. They started corresponding on a regular basis. Carl filled her in on his story and told her what he knew of her birth mother. They sent each other pictures of themselves and their family members. Typically for paranoid Carl, he put all those e-mails onto a thumb drive and locked it in a safe. To him, those first exchanges with his long-lost daughter were more precious than gold.

He didn't know what to call himself, or even whether his existence meant anything to her, but the more they chatted, the more he wanted to take it a step further. He asked her if she would mind if he just called her on the phone. He wanted to hear her voice. She said sure, and the next minute he was talking to the daughter he'd been looking for all these years.

DADDY'S GIRL

He asked if they could get together, and it just so happened she had an event at a big hotel in his area the next day. She had a couple of free hours afterward, so she said she'd be glad to meet him in person. The next day, he pulled up outside the hotel in his big Jeep, and out walked this petite, dark-haired woman, who was without a doubt Carl's daughter. She had a face just like his. He jumped out of his car, gave her an awkward hug, pulled open the passenger door, and announced he was going to take her on a magical history tour of the neighborhood where he'd grown up.

It was a good start. Carl got to show his daughter where she'd come from. She saw all the old places he and Linda used to frequent in Corona, Queens. The two hours flew by; then

Carl dropped her off at her Mercedes. Before she drove off, they hugged again, this time more warmly.

They began chatting back and forth several times a week, and Krystal invited Carl to stay with her at her condo in Florida for five days—a father-and-daughter trip so they could get to know each other better. At one point, Krystal told him she was glad he didn't have any other daughters, because she would be jealous if she wasn't his one and only. Carl was in heaven. They learned they shared the same sense of humor and the same blunt, no-BS style of communicating. They are both strong-minded and independent. When one of Carl's best buddies, who lived less than four miles from Krystal's condo, met them both, he was blown away by how similar they looked.

He was also worried. He'd never seen Carl so animated and jovial. "Carl, I gotta tell you, you don't seem like yourself," the friend said.

"What, you mean happy?"

"Yeah, but it's almost too much."

His friend had a point. When birth parents and children are first reunited, the experience can be surreal. And when that initial elation of discovering each other dies down, cracks can start to show.

While there was no doubt that he'd been the only rooster in the henhouse, Carl suggested a paternity test, just to give Krystal confirmation that he really was her father. "I wanted her to know for sure," he said.

They used a DNA testing company in Florida, where state laws make it easier to do genetic testing. They watched each other do the cheek swab, and Krystal kept her eye on Carl as he sealed the DNA evidence in an envelope. As they drove to the Federal Express office to drop of the package, she grabbed it from him to mail it herself. "I guess trust was still an issue. She didn't want me to do the old switcheroo," Carl said.

They got definitive confirmation, and the father-daughter relationship chugged along. In June, Krystal came by Carl's house to celebrate his birthday and meet his family, who by now knew all about her. They ate cake in the backyard, and Krystal gave him an iPad. A lifelong PC user, Carl was so moved by the gift that he switched to a Mac—in fact, he bought the fanciest Mac in the Apple store.

THE CRACKS

But there was still an underlying suspicion that never quite went away. One day out of the nowhere, Krystal called and started interrogating him.

"If you were looking for me so hard all those years, why don't I see your name on any of these adoption sites?" she asked him. "How hard could it have been to find me? Look at how many kids were given up for adoption in 1968."

Carl calmly pointed out that his name was posted on one of the sites. It was the third one down on the list. She clicked on it, and there was his message. She had the proof she needed that he really had been looking for her all that time.

At one point, Carl suggested they sue the city, because he felt she was wrongfully taken away from him and that her adoption wasn't legal. This got her back up a little, so he dropped the subject. Like a lot of adoptees, Krystal was feeling tremendous pressure and guilt from her adoptive family. When she confided in her sister that Carl had made contact with her, the sister flipped and told the rest of the family. Her adoptive dad was not happy. "I understand you found your real father," he said. Then he started to cry.

Carl tried to make it better for her. He wrote her adoptive father a letter, assuring him that he had no designs on taking his place, and that he was grateful to him for giving Krystal such an amazing upbringing. "I never knew what was happening," he wrote. "The birth and adoption took place without my knowledge. But she'd lived without me for forty-one years, and I would be crazy or stupid to suddenly try to be her daddy. Frankly, I don't know what I am going to be, but I guarantee you, you're her father, and her mother is her mother. Everything is going to be okay. I promise." He asked Krystal to deliver the note, and she did. But he never heard back. Krystal's family wanted nothing to do with him.

BALANCING ACT

As an adoptee myself, I understand the guilt all too well. There's a sense that if you allow this person—this birth parent—to be in your life, you are sending out a signal that you need more, that the love you were given by your adoptive family wasn't enough. Then everyone gets hurt. Even though that's not what it's really about, that's the message they get. Some adoptive families understand. But many don't. Thus you feel guilty, as if you are forsaking the family that raised you, just because you want to discover where you came from. How sad is that?

Adding to the complications for Krystal was the introduction of her birth mother into her life. I had a lead on where she was, and Carl asked me to find her. For Krystal's sake, I threw the extra service in, gratis. A few months later, I had a current last name, an address, an e-mail address, and a phone number for Linda. At first, Carl hung on to the information. He was enjoying his moment with his daughter and he was afraid the bond between birth mother and daughter would overshadow his relationship with Krystal somehow. A couple of days later, however, he passed along the information, so that Krystal could contact her if she wished.

"Kiddo, I've got the whereabouts of your birth mother if you want to contact her. It's your decision," he said.

"Really? She never looked for me. You did. Why should I bother?"

"You would have thought the same about me six months ago."

"Yeah, but what if she doesn't want to hear from me? I don't want to find out that I am being dumped twice."

"Not by me. Hey, if the worse comes to the worst, it's just you and me, kid. I'll make you a deal. I'll give you the information. Just wait six months before you do anything."

The next day, Krystal e-mailed her birth mother. A week passed, but there was no reply. Krystal even reached out to her on Facebook. Nothing. Then she got a curt message back from Linda: "Yes, that is my name. Yes, I had a child on that date. Who is this?"

When Krystal filled her in, Linda went crazy. She was so thrilled to hear from her daughter, she told everyone—her mother, who was still living with her, her husband, and her other kids. Until then, nobody had known. She'd had no plans to search for her daughter and figured she'd never see her again, so she hadn't bothered telling anyone about that episode in her past. But when her long-lost daughter reached out, she couldn't wait to see her. They met a few days later at a Panera restaurant near Holbrook, Long Island. But as Krystal was sitting there, waiting for her birth mother to show up, in waddled this obese woman who looked like a bag lady. She had missing teeth and her hair was a tangled mess. It was her birth mother.

HARD-LUCK STORY

Straightaway, she asked Krystal for a job. They talked for two hours, and Krystal learned that Linda was mad as a hatter and completely destitute. Her husband of thirty-two years, a former truck driver, had no job. He had diabetes, had lost a leg, and was on dialysis three times a week. All three of her children, who were in their thirties, were unemployed. They were on the verge of losing their home. So when Linda clapped eyes on Krystal—a well-dressed, obviously successful young woman who oozed money—she saw an opportunity.

As soon as she got home, Krystal called Carl.

"So, did you meet her?" he asked. "What did you think?"

"What did I think? What the hell were *you* thinking? It was a disaster. She's so needy. What am I going to do if she walks into my place of business?"

Carl had no idea about what Linda was like now. We later learned that Linda's life had been a series of hard knocks since she left Carl. Krystal asked her why she'd left him, and Linda told her it was because looking at him was a painful reminder of the baby girl she'd lost. Linda, her mother, and her brother moved from place to place. Linda got married and moved out, but her brother was destitute, as was their mother, so they both moved in with Linda. Linda adored her little brother, but he was trouble. When I knew him, he was a singer in a local band and the worst he did was smoke a little pot. I was no more than seventeen when I dated him, and if my parents had known I was out with a man ten years older than I was, I would have been grounded for life. He was my moment of teenage rebellion. So I was disturbed when Carl told me Linda had come home one day and found him dead in the middle of the living room floor from a drug overdose. That shock led to the first of several nervous breakdowns for Linda. I had no idea that he was involved with drugs.

Carl hadn't seen Linda since they were teenagers. He still remembered her fondly as intelligent and sweet. They'd spent three years of their lives together and—except when she disappeared to have the baby—were always on the same page. He tried to explain to Krystal that life had obviously been hard on Linda but that she was still the woman who had given birth to her, and that the woman he knew had suffered sadness and regret over giving her up. When Linda started calling Krystal incessantly, telling her she needed to meet with her to discuss an urgent matter, Carl urged his daughter to give her a second chance. "Let me tell you, I don't know what happened to her all these years. I remember a completely different person, not this crazy woman you're dealing with. We have not been in touch, but she is your mother," he said.

LAST STRAW

Krystal did meet with Linda a second time, once again going out of her way and paying for lunch. The important thing her birth mother wanted to discuss was a favor for her son, Krystal's half brother. He'd just taken the entrance exam for the New York City Fire Department, and Linda wanted Krystal's adoptive father to pull some strings for him. It was just one request after another, and it was crossing the line. Apparently life had hardened Linda and she had become calculating. She was one of life's users, determined to extract what she could from this potential gold mine. Krystal was done.

Krystal took out some of her anger and frustration on Carl. As far as she was concerned, Linda was a reflection on Carl. He'd gotten her into this, after all. Carl could sense she was pulling away from him. But he persisted. He kept up a line of communication, which was becoming increasingly one-sided. He was on a trip to Italy for his wine business when he got it into his head that he had to buy her the perfect gift for her birthday. Before his trip, he'd asked her what she wanted and she'd said nothing. But this was the first birthday since he'd met her and he was determined. He agonized about what to get her, and when he was in Bellagio on Lake Cuomo, a town known for producing the finest hand-painted silk, he asked where he could find the best. They recommended a store, and he went there and grabbed the priciest item on the shelf—an exquisite scarf.

When he got home, he called Krystal and, not wishing to impose on her actual birthday, asked if he could drop his gift off at her house the day before. Then she called him to cancel, saying she had a cold and suggesting he come by the following week. Instead, Carl sneaked up to the house and left the scarf with a card attached. That day, she called him at home. He wasn't there to take the call, but when she finally got through to him on his cell phone, the conversation was perfunctory. She thanked him, but after five minutes, it was obvious she couldn't wait to get off the phone.

"I could sense I was becoming a pain in the ass," Carl told me. "That was the last I heard from her."

The last time I spoke with Carl, he was upset. His feelings are hurt, and I guess that's understandable. "She's seen what I have done trying to find her. The least she can do is give me a call," he told me. "I got my pride. I'm not gonna be walked all over."

ROOM TO BREATHE

But Carl's overlooking an important fact. Krystal didn't ask for this. Those past forty years when he was looking for her, she had no idea. This notion of a parent who never wanted to give her up is brand-new to her. She hasn't had a lifetime to get used to it. Carl just has to be as patient as he's been persistent.

I feel for both of them; I really do. For reasons I'll get into in the next chapter, I think I know why she found it strange and suspicious that he wanted her in his life so much. His love and affection is almost frightening on some level. When you aren't searching, the person who has been looking for you and finally finds you can almost suck the life out of you. You are aware that you are the reason this person is so happy, and that you mean so much to him, and it can become burdensome. You shut down. Here is this complete stranger, and yet you are supposed to love him like a daughter loves a father, even though he has never been that person to you. You don't have that familial bond. He tells you he loves you, and it almost makes you cringe. It's a hard thing to balance. Where do you put this person in your life?

And then there's Carl. He keeps looking back to what could have been and should have been. When Linda's mother found out her daughter was pregnant, she refused, out of stubborn pride, to come forward and inform Carl's mother. She didn't want to hear her say, "I told you so." She just took the matter in her own hands, when she had no right to do so. But Carl's mother would have taken the baby in and allowed her son to raise Krystal in her home. He could have joined the police force and supported his young family. Life could have turned out very different for everyone. Wudda, cudda, shudda. It's enough to make anyone bitter.

My advice to Carl was to back off. He came on with guns a-blazin' because that's the kind of guy he is. But he has to let her come to him. It could take a few months, and may even take a few more years. She has a lot of things in her heart and mind to reconcile, including the feeling that she's being disloyal to her adoptive family. Carl has to understand that. It's not fair, but it's reality.

I've got to hand it to him. His single-minded devotion to this girl and his determination to do the right thing all these years are impressive. He's a good man. He recently shared a quote with me that's his life's motto: "The person with the greatest intensity of purpose will always prevail."

But Carl has to ease up on that intensity for now. This one is out of his hands. His wants and desires don't matter this time. All he can do is just be there for his daughter, if and when she's ready. And I think she will be, eventually. I think in time she'll come to realize there are no tricks or ulterior motives. He has nothing up his sleeve. All he has is a father's love.

The Lesson: Let It Be

Relationships cannot be forced. Reuniting is a day-by-day journey. It's complex, and it involves a gamut of emotions. Biological families have the luxury of evolving and growing up together, whereas those with newly found connections have to go through the process of trying to understand one another. It's a delicate balancing act, and if relationships are pushed too hard, they have a way of quickly dissolving.

It's hard to know when you are crossing someone's boundaries when you truly don't know that person. I personally have gone through the same highs and lows with my sisters, and I am learning when to pull back and when to push forward. But it's not without months of not speaking or the occasional arguments and misunderstandings.

Typically, the person searching has had the fantasy in his mind for so long of what the relationship is supposed to be like, and if he doesn't adapt to reality, it can go south. When the person who's done the searching is not received with an equal amount of excitement by the person who has been found, it often feels like a rejection, and that has been the case with Carl. It doesn't matter what happened in the past; Krystal has loyalties to another family. We as searchers need to be patient. We need to take a deep breath, step back, and try to understand.

CHAPTER EIGHT

Vinnie on the Corner

◆ ◆ ◆

Growing up, I never really wondered about my birth father. Clearly, I was obsessed with finding my birth mother, which proved to have disastrous results. It seems as though the majority of my clients feel the same way I do. Perhaps we hold some resentment for our biological fathers. If they had stepped up to the plate and done the right thing by our birth mothers, would the adoptions have ever taken place? There is just something about the birth-mother bond that can't compare. Although the truth is that most birth fathers were never given an opportunity to participate in making plans for their baby's future.

Besides, my father had long since passed away and I felt a strong allegiance to him. I just wasn't ready for another paternal figure in my life. My dad married my mother—his childhood sweetheart—when he was twenty. He worked hard his whole life, sick or not. As a teenager, my dad suffered an injury to his leg that infected the bone and stopped its growth. He was five feet eight when it happened, but the rest of him grew to be six two, so he had to wear an orthopedic shoe with a six-inch platform. He didn't walk with a limp, but when we were out in public and I caught people staring, I wanted to tear their eyes out. My dad was my first love. I was in awe of his dignity and patience. He also suffered from what we now know was lupus, but throughout my father's painful illness, he went every day to his job as a funeral director and never once complained. He supported his family, and gave my brother and me everything we needed, and more. He was crazy about my mother and doted on her until the day he died, at age fifty-four. Faithful, loving, with a clear sense of right and wrong, he went out of his way to help other people, and he was always my guiding light. So finding my birth father wasn't nearly as important as finding my birth mother, as is the case for most adoptees.

But the stakes changed when Priscilla threw the stink bomb of my paternity into my lap. Her insinuation that I was the product of incest made me determined to prove her wrong. Maybe her father did rape her. I have no idea. But my gut told me it was more likely a twisted lie meant to inflict the greatest possible pain—my punishment for daring to contact her.

A few months after my toxic exchange with Priscilla, I called the agency that handled my adoption and read them the riot act. I told them that if there was any chance that what Priscilla had said was true, it meant they'd lied to me and jeopardized the health of my children. If they were willingly withholding information I needed to know about my father, there'd be trouble. I was getting ready to lawyer up. They assured me they had already told me as much as they knew, and that the information was accurate. My birth father's first name was Vinnie, and, coincidentally, given my adoptive father's profession as an undertaker, he worked in the Bronx as a mortician.

I had to find this guy. I was a raging maniac. I phoned every morgue and funeral parlor in the book. Finally, one guy answered the phone and said, "You must mean Big Vinnie! He works over at Lincoln Hospital."

I called their human resources department and got an angel on the other end of the phone. She'd just helped her best friend find her birth parents. She told me she was there for me, and that she'd get back to me after she'd made a few calls on my behalf. It turned out that Vinnie was out on disability for a bad back, but she tracked him down, and half an hour later I got the call.

"This is Big Vinnie. I hear you're lookin' for me."

I thought to myself, *God, if my birth mother wasn't bad enough, now I have the mob on the line.*

"Hi, Vinnie. I don't know how to tell you this. . . ."

"Just lay it on the line, sweetheart."

"Well, my birth mother's name is Priscilla and—"

"Cupcake, I know who you are. You're my daughter. You were born on my birthday."

"When was that?"

"February twenty-third."

"Right!"

"Come on over. Your grandmother wants to see you. We'll get cannoli, we'll sit down, and we'll talk."

That night, my husband and I drove to Vinnie's neighborhood, a very rough area of the Bronx. He met us on a nearby street corner and walked us over to his building, to make sure we didn't get mugged on the way. He wasn't exactly the tall and strapping young Lothario I'd envisioned. Instead, he was hunched over and looked much older than his fifty years. He'd obviously had a hard life.

I PRAYED FOR YOU

As we made our way up the five flights of stairs to the small tenement apartment he shared with his mother, he told us how he'd lived in that building since his own father left him at the age of two. When we walked in, the first thing I noticed were lines of boric acid powder along the doorways to keep away the cockroaches. Then Vinnie's mother—my grandmother— came out of the bedroom crying and gave me a huge hug.

"I prayed for you girls all these years!" she said.

I awkwardly returned her embrace. It was a lot to take in all at once and I was distracted.

"Wait a minute—girls? What do you mean, 'girls'?"

"Don't you know? You have a sister!"

Vinnie told me that my mother was already pregnant with my sister at the time she gave me up. We were born eleven months apart. Then Priscilla gave away my sister. I've found this is not unusual for birth mothers. They tend to want to replace the child they just lost, but their circumstances don't change, so they go through all the trauma of relinquishing the next child as well.

LOTHARIO

Truth be told, I was a little repelled by Vinnie at first. That father-daughter bond didn't come naturally to me. At one point in our meeting, I asked to see some pictures of Priscilla when she was young. Vinnie told me I looked just like her, and I wanted to see for myself. He went into the other room and brought out an old shoe box. It was full of pictures . . . of various women. There must have been hundreds in there. Vinnie was such a player. For a moment, I felt sorry for Priscilla. She was one in a string of Vinnie's conquests. He couldn't have been less like the man who raised me.

And yet Vinnie readily acknowledged me as his biological daughter. He welcomed me into his home and he was touched that I'd tried so hard to find him. He told me he'd thought about me *and my sister* all these years, and he'd always wondered how we were doing. Vinnie never married. He was one of these guys who could never commit. And yet he did do right by his son, Vincent, another child he had out of wedlock (I am assuming there are only three of us). When he was just a young boy, Vincent's mother died of cancer. Vinnie finally stepped up to the plate as a father and took him in. Vinnie and his mother raised Vincent (who also goes by Vinnie), and they did well by the kid. Vincent—my baby brother—is twenty-eight at the time of writing this, and I think he has a bright future. I don't know him as a brother, but I really like him. He's intelligent and educated. He went to graduate school, and now he's doing what he can to find a full-time job on Wall Street.

I'm almost certain I share Vinnie senior's DNA. We don't look exactly alike, but when I see pictures of Vinnie side by side with my son Ronnie, there's a definite resemblance. When he was a baby—at the time I first met Vinnie—my son was platinum blond, so I didn't see it back then. But now it's unmistakable. They even have the same wavy dark blond hair.

No, it wasn't the ideal father-daughter reunion. But it was what I needed at the time. It was such a relief to know the sordid story my birth mother told me wasn't true, and confirmation that Priscilla was a truly sick woman. When I found out the real story, I was irate. As soon as I got home, I called Priscilla.

"Guess what I found out. I met my birth father. He told me everything. I know that I have a little sister. I don't know why you did what you did to me. It was despicable. I can't believe you put me through that!"

Once again, she hung up on me. Then three days later, at eight o'clock in the morning, I got a call. The voice on the other end was like ice. "This is your mother," she said.

Dear God, I thought, this most definitely is NOT my mother. "You know what, Priscilla," I said. "You win. I'm done. It's over. Go on with your life. I wish you well."

"Not so fast. You made me think about things I never wanted to think about again. I'm going to kill you."

This time, I really was done. I'd finally reached a point where I decided it wasn't worth it.

My lifelong search for my birth mother ended in spectacular failure. It was not the happy ending that 90 percent of my clients get to experience. But at least it gave me a relationship with my birth father, sort of. That's been a mixed blessing.

After my initial contact with Vinnie, I didn't see him again for more than a decade. My adoptive father had raised the bar so high that Vinnie somehow fell short. And, frankly, my few exchanges with him made me feel a little squeamish. As was the case with Carl and his daughter, this is not a bond that can be forced. There's no history there. And our value system is so different.

We spoke sporadically over the years, but when Vinnie tried to express any kind of paternal affection, it made me uneasy. Whenever he'd say "I love you, sweetheart," I would literally squirm. And then there were times when Vinnie would be completely inappropriate. He had a tendency to make tasteless remarks, which made the hairs on the back of my neck stand up.

And that was the least of it. Besides being grotesquely off-color sometimes, Vinnie started backpedaling a little on whether or not I was actually his biological daughter. He said he simply couldn't say for sure. He could be very sweet, protective, and paternal one minute, and creepy and cavalier the next. It was confusing. After the sucker punch I got from my birth mother, I decided I just couldn't handle a relationship with Vinnie, so I distanced myself.

But a year ago, the old nagging doubt came back again. I decided I wanted to know once and for all if Vinnie was my biological father. I asked him if he'd mind taking a DNA test with me.

"Anything for you, doll. I just wish you'd call me more often," he said.

"I'll do better than that, Vinnie. I'll come see you," I replied.

TOO MUCH MOZZARELLA

The intervening years had not been kind to him. He'd gained one hundred pounds since I'd seen him last. He was six feet five and weighed 375 pounds. He could barely walk, and only with a cane. He had diabetes and his feet were purple. He was about to lose a foot. He looked way older than his sixty-six years. His son told me he eats salami, prosciutto, mozzarella, and Entenmann's cakes all day long. The man almost certainly had clogged arteries. I didn't even know all the things that were wrong with him. If he made it another year, I'd have been shocked.

Vinnie was his usual hospitable self. He laid out a huge spread for me and Mike. He's all about feeding the ones he loves—another sign we are related. We chatted for a while, but I was still uncomfortable in his presence. And there was something even more forlorn about the atmosphere of his home without his mother—my grandmother.

We did our DNA swabs and I sealed our evidence in separate envelopes before posting the test kit back to the lab. Weeks later, the results came back: "Inconclusive." It happens sometimes, or so we were told. It's not a perfect science. So we went through the process again. The next time, it got weirder. The lab manager called me to ask if it was possible we'd switched our samples. According to the test, I had the DNA of a man and Vinnie had the DNA of a woman.

"I might have broad shoulders, but I can assure you I am all female," I told her. "And Vinnie sure isn't some hermaphrodite!"

Clearly, these guys were totally incompetent. I didn't trust their results. I contemplated visiting my biological grandfather's daughter in Baltimore to do a DNA test with her. I wanted to rule out the specter of my birth mother's nasty insinuation altogether. But the more time passes, the less I care. I don't know that I want to do it anymore, or that I need the scientific evidence. I don't think it matters now. With every pore of my being, I now feel like Vinnie must be my birth father. The more I get to know him, the more I see what we have in common. We share the same warped sense of humor. We don't pull any punches. We have the same no-BS style. Good or bad, people always know where they stand with us. On some strange level, we get each other. Vinnie has grown on me.

GOODFELLA

I first started to appreciate his sincerity about a year ago, when Priscilla contacted him out of the blue. Evidently, she was paranoid that we'd been in communication, and she'd seen a few things on the Internet and on television about what I do for a living. She wanted to poke around and get the goods on me from Vinnie. But Priscilla is a manipulator, and Vinnie knows it. He confirmed she'd had a hard life, and that the circumstances that led to my being given up for adoption had been tough on her. But he made no apology for who she is today. He didn't like what she was up to. His loyalty was to me. His first response was to call me and give me a heads-up and let me know that I might be receiving another harassing phone call. He was right. The games continued. One minute, she'd lash out and tell me I was nothing to her (which was fine by me); the next minute, she'd try to send indirect messages that she was a poor victim who needed my financial help.

Her last call to Vinnie was much more explicit. He was so upset for me, and angry at Priscilla, he tried frantically to call me. When he finally got through, he said, "Sweetheart, I have to tell you something."

"What's going on, Vinnie?"

"I ripped your birth mother a new one. She wanted me to contact you."

"What for?"

"Because she wanted me to ask you for money."

"Are you kidding me?"

"She laid on some sob story that you're living in this fancy house with a successful television show and you just cut her off. I wasn't having any of it. I told her, 'That kid has been trying to reach out to you for fifteen years. Now that you know she's doing good, you want to know her? I'm telling you now, Don't bother her!'"

"Thanks, Vinnie!"

"Baby girl, I was never going to step into something between you and her, but I told her I think what she's doing is disgusting. I tore her up."

It suddenly occurred to me that Vinnie was being fatherly. A little protective instinct came out when he'd heard from Priscilla. I was touched. His armor has come down, and my own hesitation about getting to know him better has lessened over time. He's not inappropriate with me anymore. He's changing. When he talks to me he sounds like, well, a dad.

As for Priscilla, I feel as though I am healed. The lesson that I have learned is to accept people for who they are. No matter how much I wanted to love her, I could not change her. I cannot help but conclude that she is not someone I would have welcomed into my life under any circumstances after learning what she's all about. I told Vinnie I no longer had a need or use for her in my life. Her motives for reaching out to me were not genuine.

Besides, I *had* a mother, and she was a wonderful, loving woman. When she was unexpectedly and unnecessarily ripped away from me, Priscilla and everything my birth mother once meant to me at one point in my life receded into a big black void.

My adoptive mother had been having knee problems, but otherwise she was in great health. Her diabetes was under control. She was active. She was getting a series of injections in her knee to create a cushion for the joints, and the therapy was working fine. But on the third treatment, she developed a massive hematoma. Her doctor decided to operate and relieve some of the pressure building up under her kneecap. But I had my doubts. He'd already messed up once, so who was to say he wouldn't mess up again?

She had the surgery anyway and they sent her home with some OxyContin. They didn't even put a pressure bandage on her leg. Mom spent an uncomfortable first night, but during her second day she was starting to feel better. I took her some blankets, cooked for her, and generally made her feel comfortable. We weren't all huggy and kissy, my mom and I. We just showed affection by teasing each other and joking around. I made fun of all the crocheted blankets in her room and propped her up with some more pillows. Then, the next morning, she complained of dizziness. She had no pain, but she felt funny. I was ready to call a doctor, but she insisted she was fine. I figured it was the pain meds, so I threw them away. Then she started struggling for breath. Despite her protests, I called an ambulance, and it seemed like a lifetime before they came. By the time the medics burst into Mom's room, she was slumped against me. They had to tear me away from her. Then it was all a blur. I just remember banging on the door to be let back in, and when I finally got the door open, she was coding. They had her on the floor with the paddles out, frantically working to revive her. Sadly, my mother continued to code over and over again on the way to the hospital and at the hospital. A blood clot had traveled to her heart and caused a massive coronary. They couldn't save her, and I don't think Mom ever regained consciousness after that first time she fell against me. In the space of twenty-five minutes, it was over. Once again, I was an orphan.

THE GREATEST LOSS

That's truly how I feel now. I miss her so much. I know everyone says it, but you never realize how precious someone is until you lose them. There are so many things you wish you could do over again. One of the most painful things for me is the memory of my mother's insecurity about my own search for birth relatives. About a week before she died, she overheard that Priscilla was trying to contact me, and she got worried. It made me so mad!

"Ma, how could you?" I snapped at her. "How could you possibly think that I would ever try to replace you? Don't you know how much you mean to me? How is it that you could doubt my feelings for you for even a second?"

Even though we weren't sentimental, my mom had become much more affectionate later in life, and now I wish I'd been more that way with her. I wish a lot of things. I don't have the same regrets regarding my dad, because he died over a period of a week. We were able to say all the things we wanted to say. Same with Ronnie, my brother. He was sick for a long time. But losing my mother has been brutal. When I had something to share, she was always the person I'd run to first, even before my husband. Part of me thinks this is temporary, and that I can just tell her later, when she comes back. It just doesn't feel real. Mom was living with us for years, and she was a part of the fabric of our lives. She made our house a home and prepared all the meals. She always sat at the head of the table. And now she's left me alone in this frat house of boys. At forty-six years old, after two kids and more than twenty years of marriage, I have been forced to become an adult, and I sure don't feel like one. To this day, nobody sits in my mother's chair.

Vinnie didn't know any of this until weeks after it happened. He'd never met the woman who raised me, although he would have loved to. When I told him my news, he was upset that I'd waited so long to do so.

"You're telling me now? Cupcake, why the hell didn't you call me?"

"Oh Vinnie, I don't know. There's been so much going on, it's just hard to talk about. And you've got your own problems."

"Pammie, I'm here for you twenty-four/seven. I don't care about the DNA test. I was the first person to see you when you were born. I was with you when you were still in Priscilla's belly."

It was in that defining moment I realized this guy was the only person on earth who'd known me as a baby—or at least the only person who mattered. It sounds weird, but that really meant something. When you are adopted, you lose six months to a year of your life. Growing up, there is no one around who has a memory of who you were as this tiny person. It's a no-man's-land in your life story. Who cared for you? Who saw you? Who made sure you were fed and changed and held? To have that connection with another human being—someone who knows about your existence from birth really adds something to your life on a level I don't think even I can fully comprehend yet.

There's something oddly comforting knowing Vinnie is that person in my life. There's a tender heart under all those crude Vinnie Goumba defenses he puts up. As we were talking, he kept saying he loved me, and I noticed it no longer made me flinch.

"Every journey starts with one step, and you've been on quite a journey. I'm so proud of you, kiddo, and you're doing so good," he said. "Don't let anyone take that away from you."

I asked him how he was doing. He'd had some bad luck lately. His disability payments weren't keeping up with his expenses. He had a second home in Westchester, but he couldn't pay the mortgage anymore. Vinnie junior has three degrees, but he'd lost his job, so he couldn't contribute. The kid has hustle, but he's in the same boat as everyone else. So the pair of them were really struggling. But he didn't share those troubles with me until after the fact.

"Aw, Vinnie, I'm so sorry! I know how much you loved that place."

"What are you sorry for me for, sweetheart? I'm not sorry. I got food on my table and a roof over my head. There is somebody out there worse off than me. There is always somebody out there who's got it worse than you."

"Wow, Vin! You're full of a lot of wisdom today. You should put that on a Hallmark card!

"My wisdom is reserved only for the people I love, because I had to learn the hard way. I don't want the people I love to learn the hard way."

His health was getting worse, so I nagged him to take care of it, acting like, well, a daughter. He was going downhill fast, and I was afraid he might be dying.

"Ah, who gives a crap? I'm ready to go."

"No, Vinnie, don't say that! What about your son? With you and his grandmother gone, he'll have no one."

"He's a grown man."

"Take it from me, Vinnie, It doesn't matter if you're six or forty-six, you always need your parents. It's never easy to lose a mother or father. Try to hang on a little longer, for your son's sake."

It was then I realized I wasn't just speaking for Vinnie junior. I was speaking for myself. We may not be living out the father-daughter fairy tale, but it matters to me that he exists. On some strange but profound level, I care about this man and I'm not ready to lose him, too. In his own dysfunctional way, he is nurturing and kind. The DNA test means nothing to me now, because I know the blood tie is real. I still don't know exactly where my birth father fits into my life. It's something adoptees struggle with for years. I just hope Vinnie sticks around long enough for me to figure it out.

The Lesson: It Is What It Is

The pivotal moment for my relationship with Vinnie was when I realized he was the only person in my life who knew me when I was born. That knowledge somehow made me feel more connected to him.

Vinnie will never be my idea of a father, because I had a father, and that wonderful man died long ago. That's not to say that I don't have room for Vinnie in my life. I think he has a good heart, and although he is not the person I was raised to view as a father figure, there is a kindness and compassion in him that has won me over.

Don't make the mistake of having unrealistic expectations of people. Not everyone is able to live up to your idea of what they are supposed to be in your life. Relationships eventually work when you allow people to be who they are and not what you expect them to be. The label of mother or father comes with great meaning. Even though you may feel a connection to your birth parent immediately, it takes great understanding, patience, and work to cultivate these newly formed relationships.

Bear in mind that you are forming relationships with complete strangers. I like to tell my clients to treat reunions like they are dating: one date at a time. Get to know each other slowly. Respect each other's boundaries.

The triad experience can leave us with a set of insecurities that makes us especially needy. Acknowledge your own needs and allow others to breathe. It will happen the way it's supposed to, just you wait and see.

CHAPTER NINE

The Level Playing Field

• • •

There's something about finding that connection with our long-lost brothers and sisters that allows us to breathe. Unlike the guilt and conflicting mess of emotions that can weigh down our relationships with our birth parents, siblings exist on a level playing field. All is fair in this reunion. We didn't ask to be put on this earth. It wasn't our decision that one child was kept and another was given up. Sure, there's baggage, just like there is in any relationship, but it's lighter. And, through our brothers and sisters, whether they are full-blood or half-blood, we gain a richer understanding about ourselves and where we came from, even when we don't get to have that long-sought meeting with our birth mother or father. It's why I make a point of always trying to find a brother or sister for my clients, especially when it's too late and their birth mother has already passed. It takes away some of the sting of disappointment and gives back something more. Our siblings help us fill in the missing pieces and complete that first chapter with recognition, acceptance, friendship and, eventually, love.

One of the happier outcomes of my disastrous reunion with my birth mother was discovering that I had a sister. I was stunned to learn from Vinnie that there were two of us. But how would I find her? I couldn't afford to hire another private detective, so I had to figure out a way to search for her myself. This was my baptism as a searcher. I was terrified of another rejection, but the knowledge that I had a sister pushed me forward. I'd never had a sister, and the thought of connecting with a woman my age who shared my DNA thrilled me. My adoptive brother had been gone a long time, and there were no other siblings in the family that raised me. I *had* to meet her. Luckily, I had the help of my adoptee comrade Lydia. She taught me where to look first.

In New York City, there's a list of every child born between the years 1890 and 1984. I was born Roberta Wade, and I found another fifteen females under the name of Wade born between 1965 and 1966. Again, I was on a mission. I called every one of them, begging for information. I called the appropriate adoption agency for clues, and learned how to ask leading questions that would get me the information I needed while not getting the person at the other end of the phone into trouble. I also got better at listening between the lines: *No, not her, and not her, either; you might want to explore that further. . . .*

BLOOD BOND

Four months later, I met the woman who had been born Charlene Wade—my sister Kathy. We'd already spoken on the phone a few times by then. When I first called her, she was in the middle of her son's first birthday party and it was hectic.

"Hello, Kathy? My name is Pamela Slaton. I am searching for someone who was born with the last name of Wade and was adopted. Could this person be you? I have to talk to you about something important."

"Look, I think I know what this is about, but I'm sorry, I can't right now. It's my little guy's special day. . . ."

She went on to explain that she was stressing out about dinner and had to run out and pick up the birthday cake.

"Oh, I totally understand. I have two little guys myself. Please call me back when you can. We'll talk then," I said.

For the next few hours, I kept my fingers crossed. I didn't

necessarily get the sense that she wouldn't call me back, although it's stressful when the person you are searching for puts you off for a day or two. It makes you wonder if she'll back out of making the connection once the shock of that phone call hits.

Kathy learned she was adopted when she was eleven, but she had no idea she might have a sibling out there somewhere. Her adopted parents never said much about it, although they must have known. They admitted that she was adopted only when a neighbor let something slip. When she found out, she let it lie. Not everyone has the desire to search. On the one occasion she questioned her father about it, he asked her if it made her feel any different about him. Of course it didn't. She'd been with her parents since she was three days old, and as far as she was concerned, if her birth mother and father weren't looking for her, she should leave it alone. It was one thing we didn't have in common.

But when Kathy did call me back later that day, our connection was instant. There was nothing awkward or stilted about our phone conversation. It wasn't like we were two complete strangers trying to force ourselves to catch up over a lifetime. I told her everything I'd learned about our birth family. She was shocked. It turned out that the whole time Kathy was growing up, Priscilla, our birth mother, lived just a few miles away, with a cousin who'd raised her. Priscilla's parents had divorced and each of the children had been raised by a different family member—a big part of the reason why my birth mother's life's path took the direction it did.

This cousin, who was more like an aunt to Kathy, often used to come over to her house to visit. But when I told Kathy the situation, it dawned on her that she never actually went over to the cousin's house. In fact, when her parents dropped this cousin off in the car, it was always around the corner—they never even drove past Priscilla's house. When Kathy checked her adoptive mother's black address book, she even found Priscilla's number. Her birth mother had been right there under her nose all along.

TWIN FEET

I couldn't wait to meet Kathy in person. I decided to surprise her. She was flying into La Guardia from a Florida vacation with her boyfriend, so I convinced the airline to tell me which flight she was on. I met her as soon as she came out of the gate. (It was long before 9/11 security precautions.)

I wasn't fooling anyone. Kathy walked straight up to me. She knew me right away. We all sat down, she and her boyfriend and my husband and I, and it was as if we'd known each other our whole lives. Our one-liners bounced back and forth like balls in a tennis volley. We shared the same twisted sense of humor. We were both tall and had long blond hair that we hated to cut, and we both looked like our birth mother. We took our shoes off to compare our misshapen baby toes, which were exactly alike.

UNITED FRONT

Over the next year, we started taking family trips together. Kathy has three kids, and her eldest son is the same age as my youngest. Those two—Johnny and my Mikey—bonded right away. My son loved having a cousin to run around with, and our Fourth of July weekends at Lake George, in upstate New York, have become sacred to those boys. Kathy and I are both fans of the beach, and we always try to spend at least a week together at a beach house on Long Beach Island, on the Jersey shore. We connect as moms. Most of the time, my husband, our kids, and her boyfriend are around, but one of the first moments we truly felt like sisters was when we realized two of our boys had sneaked out at 12:30 in the morning. We were fuming, and nervous, but we knew they had to be somewhere close by, so we grabbed a bottle of wine and a couple of lawn chairs and camped out on our driveway, waiting. We joked about that "gotcha" moment when our sons would turn up, and how we would greet them with our arms folded—a United Front of Angry Motherhood. Our kids did eventually turn up, looking appropriately sheepish about breaking the rules. I was glad not to have to go through that ordeal alone.

Kathy and I live in the same state but are separated by a two-and-a-half-hour drive. Aside from the occasional get-together and family event, we aren't a regular part of each other's lives. Kathy is a single mom, and she's busy. We both have crazy schedules, so it's not always easy to get together and maintain that sisterly bond. We'll often meet halfway so our sons can get together, but those moments for just the two of us are rare. One weekend, we decided we needed to have a girls' night out with no husband or boyfriend, so we took off for Atlantic City. It was a laugh riot from the minute we checked into the hotel room. Kathy is the sort of girl I would have partied with in college, whether or not we were related. We both know how to have a good time. On that level, we are the same. We did the usual—cocktails, dinner, gambling, more cocktails—but it was the way we could joke around and find the humor in every little thing that made the weekend memorable. Well, what we could remember of it anyway. It doesn't take much to make either of us tipsy, but we can handle three drinks each, and that's all we had. Someone must have slipped a roofie in our cocktails while we weren't looking, because when we woke up in our hotel room the next morning, we were both sick as dogs, with no idea how in the hell we'd gotten back there the previous night. Our throats were dry and we had rocks in our heads. We could barely move.

"Whatever happened, please tell me we used protection," I joked.

As sick as we were, we both laughed like hell. It was like a scene out of *The Hangover Part III*.

WORK IN PROGRESS

But for all our similarities, there are some fundamental differences. We weren't raised together. We didn't share a room. Our upbringings were as different as night and day. Kathy's dad died when she was eleven, shortly after she found out she was adopted. Her mother became ill when Kathy was still a child, and Kathy ended up being her main caregiver. She was forced to grow up quickly, and she was pretty much robbed of her childhood. She didn't have any brothers or sisters to share the burden; there were no older role models to share their wisdom; she had no one to trust or to confide in. Kathy learned how to parent herself at a young age and she is very independent. She trusts only herself, which, in turn, has often caused me to withdraw from her. Our relationship is still very much a work in progress.

We had our first big blowout about a year ago. It was getting close to our Fourth of July weekend, but I hadn't heard from her in a while. It was probably something I'd said. I love my sister, but I get frustrated with the choices she makes. Some of the men in her life have been bad news, and as one who's naturally outspoken in my opinions, I let her know what I think. Kathy listens, agrees, then goes ahead and continues to make the same mistakes over and over again. Maybe this is the dynamic between a lot of older and younger sisters. But Kathy shuts down for a while. I decided that just because we were on the outs, we shouldn't deprive Mikey and Johnny of each other's company, so I reached out to her.

"Hey, Kathy! How are you? It's not going to be the same going to Lake George without your little guy, so whaddaya say?"

"Pammie! That sounds good to me. And funny you should call, because I just had surgery."

"You what? Why didn't you tell me? What happened?"

"I had a hernia operation and I've been stuck on the couch in agony for weeks."

I made light of it, but I was actually a little hurt that she hadn't told me earlier. She's my sister, after all, and I thought sisters were supposed to share important stuff like that. It was always up to me to call and find out. I would gladly have gone to see her and helped out. But as always, by telling me after the fact, she didn't allow me the opportunity to be there for her. There have been so many major things in Kathy's life that she hasn't shared with me since we reunited. She clams up, and it's frustrating. I realize now it's just Kathy's way. She's used to keeping these things to herself. She's done it her whole life. But at the time, it made me wonder how we were ever going to get closer as siblings.

Kathy's evasiveness with me recently caused one of our arguments to get out of control. It went on for hours. We got right into the gutter. We are both levelheaded women until our tempers flare. We said things to each other that I have never dared say to anyone else. In a weird way, I was amused that she could be just as nasty as I could be. When we fight, we go for the jugular, and nothing is off-limits. We now call it "unleashing our inner Priscillas." There's obviously something genetic inside each of us that can turn nasty when we're pushed too far. Only Kathy could argue with me like that. We slowly started mending fences. In a funny way, I think it made us closer. For some inexplicable reason, we are drawn to each other; we seem to need each other in our lives. Maybe it's because we both know we are all we have.

FOUR BLONDES

About two years ago, I also made the connection with our half sisters. My relationship with these siblings is even trickier than my dysfunctional bond with Kathy. They were raised by Priscilla and, by their own accounts, it was not a happy upbringing. Priscilla had been busy, popping out seven kids over her lifetime, myself and Kathy included, but I reached out to only two sisters. Two of my siblings are so troubled, I was warned by one of the sisters with whom I am in contact to stay away. It's a world I just don't have the strength to step into.

Years ago, before I met Vinnie, I tracked down Diana (I won't use my half sisters' real names). She was in the middle of a breakup and moving to a new house, and my call came at precisely the wrong time. She freaked out, told me she wasn't ready to talk and that she'd call me back. Then she proceeded to lose my number. It wasn't until two years ago, when I randomly decided to do an Internet search on my other sister—whom I'll call Lisa—that we finally managed to meet. The Google search brought up a link to her Facebook page, and when I saw her picture, I nearly fell off my chair. She looked exactly the way I had twenty years ago. I couldn't resist the temptation, so I sent her a friend request. When I reached out, she was thrilled to hear from me, and furious with Diana for keeping my initial phone call a secret for so long.

When we spoke, Lisa told me she was excited but afraid. She suffers from anxiety, and she didn't know if, when the final hour came, she'd have the guts to meet me. I wasn't accepting that as an excuse.

"But Lisa, I am your sister."

"No, you don't understand."

"Yes, I do. My son suffers from anxiety."

I was learning more. There's a thread of anxiety that runs

throughout this family. It explains a lot about my own panic attacks.

Finally, Lisa agreed to meet. She told Diana, and I told Kathy, and we dragged them along to a little Irish pub in Southern New Jersey. Kathy said what she always says when I pursue our blood relatives: "I'll go along for the ride, but you're driving."

We sat down at one in the afternoon and finished at nine. The owner himself was adopted, and he was fascinated by our story. The food and drinks kept coming. It was one of the best times I've had in my life. We didn't feel like strangers. On some level, it was very familiar, as if we'd always known one another.

VOICE FROM THE PAST

About a year after our reunion, I got a call from someone I hadn't heard from in years. My life was hectic because I was in the middle of production for my television show, so I wasn't home when the phone rang on my business line. She left a message: "I am trying to reach Pam. I am calling on behalf of her mother. I'll try again later."

I thought it must have been someone from our church trying to get a hold of my adoptive mother, so I didn't think much of it. Then there was another voice mail: "I have information about Pam's mother. I'll be calling back soon."

The blood drained from my head. I thought something must have happened to Mom. Had she fallen? Was she okay? I didn't realize she was at home, but she was there in her room the whole time. She was fine.

That night in bed, Mike asked me if the caller could have been Priscilla.

"No way! That's over," I said.

But I couldn't put it out of my mind. The next morning, I called Diana. She'd grown up with Priscilla, so she'd be sure to recognize her voice, I figured. I played her the message and held the cell phone up to the machine.

"Yep, that's her," Diana said.

"What could she possibly want?"

"God knows, Pam. I haven't talked to her in ages."

Two hours later, my phone rang, and it was Priscilla, all sweetness and light, as usual.

"What's up Priscilla? What's going on?" I asked.

"Somebody told me to call you."

"Who?"

"Somebody. It's not important who."

"Frankly, Priscilla, I am a little shocked by this call, because it's my understanding you don't like me."

"Well, I don't."

"Okay, then. Um, so why don't you let me know how I can help you?"

"Are you friends with my daughters?"

"You mean my sisters?"

"No, my daughters. Those aren't your sisters."

"I don't know what you're talking about, Priscilla. Where I come from, if people are born of the same mother, it makes them siblings."

"Okay, your half sisters. Are you friends with them?"

"Yes, I know them. So what's this about?"

"You want to get in my life that bad?"

"This has nothing to do with you. I have the right to know who they are."

"Oh, so you're punishing me."

"Again, Priscilla, my relationship with my sisters has nothing to do with you. Let me make it perfectly clear. If you think I am still vying for your love and attention, you are wrong. I am over it and I am over you. I don't know what I can help you with, but the truth of the matter is, I have no interest."

"Wait a minute—"

"Let me finish. And when you referred to calling about my mother on those phone messages, it could not have been further from the truth. My mother is standing right here in my kitchen, cooking dinner."

Then Priscilla started to laugh, but there was no humor in her laughter. It was more like a bitter cackle.

"Priscilla, I don't know what I can say to you at this point."

"Don't bother my daughters. They don't want to know you."

"That's for them to decide. I am sure they'll tell me if they don't want to see me."

I called my sisters afterward, and they were horrified, although not surprised. They'd never even discussed me with Priscilla, and they assumed their mother must have seen that we were Facebook friends. They told me Priscilla almost never wanted to have anything to do with her kids, unless she needed them for some reason. Lisa told me her mother had been downright cruel to her. "Mom says 'family' when it's convenient," she told me.

Hearing what their lives were like growing up with our birth mother made my heart ache for my little sisters. I felt a mixture of sadness and relief that I was the lucky one. I'd gotten out undamaged.

I love those girls. Knowing them completes me. But it's not all perfect. I've had to learn to put my expectations of sisterhood away in a box, because the loyalty, trust, and unconditional love I hoped for in a sibling relationship simply does not flick on like a switch. My sisters run hot and cold, caught up in their own problems and resentments, which have nothing to do with me. They want to see me, but on their terms. They are sweethearts, and from what they've shared with me about the neglect and sadness of their childhoods, it's amazing that they've turned out as lovely, funny, and caring as they have. But there are times when I feel like our relationship is too one-sided, and these days, I don't have the strength to carry it all.

THE REAL THING

I know what real closeness with a sibling is like. I felt a connection to my adopted brother Ronnie, from the time I was an infant. I was ten months old when my parents brought me home, and I couldn't stop crying. I was traumatized by being in this new place with these new faces, and I screamed my head off, until I first laid eyes on my brother. He was the only one who could get me to calm down. When we were little, we played together all the time. I called him "Sweetie Boy" and he called me "Maga"—which was his way of saying "Grandma." I was two years younger than Ronnie, but he used to let me boss him around as if I were his older sister. When it was playtime, I was in charge.

We grew apart as teenagers, which can happen in the closest of families. I was the smart-mouthed rebel and Ronnie was the golden boy who always tried to do the right thing. He was studious, conservative, and athletic. He played center on our high school football team. We were like oil and vinegar. He disapproved of my party-girl ways, and he definitely wasn't with me in my desire to search for my birth parents. He didn't even want to discuss it.

When Ronnie was nineteen, he started complaining about a problem in his knee. We assumed it was an old football injury, so my parents took him to a top orthopedic surgeon in Manhattan. He told us it was probably water on the knee or some kind of cartilage damage and that he'd have to operate. Ronnie had the surgery and we took him back home to Queens with his leg inside a cast. Two days later, Ronnie woke up in the middle of the night, screaming in agony and running a high fever. Fearing his leg was infected, we rushed him to the hospital, where they cut off the cast and saw something that just didn't look right. When they opened up my brother's leg again, they saw a tumor the size of a softball. The lump had grown that much in forty-eight hours. My brother was diagnosed with bone cancer, and it was the worst kind. No amount of chemo would be able to shrink the tumor enough, because part of it was in the artery. The only way to prevent it from spreading was to amputate the leg from the thigh down. This beautiful, athletic boy had to lose his leg.

By then, Ronnie and I had reconciled. I was just seventeen, but my brother's illness forced me to grow up fast. I grew protective of him, more like an older sister. Come to think of it, I always was. I remember a couple of boys were threatening to beat him up once, when we were younger, and I got so worried for him. He was quiet and he lacked my street smarts. If anyone looked at him the wrong way, that person would have me to deal with.

Ronnie went into remission for a year, but his hair fell out from the chemo and he was so thin. I went shopping for him and bought him cool clothes. One night, we went out to the club together. Ronnie never got used to his prosthetic leg, so he left it at home and used his crutches. He didn't care. He just hobbled in with his head held high, but I was watching his back the whole time. He was always surrounded by friends. When he was going through the treatment, they'd all come to the house and just sit for hours watching TV with him. They were by his side when he threw up, and when he was too weak to lift his head off the pillow. He was so loved in the neighborhood.

SIXTH SENSE

For a while, we thought he was getting better. We allowed ourselves to hope that he'd beaten his cancer. Then one afternoon, I had an asthma attack. I didn't have asthma, but that's what it felt like. My chest was heaving and I couldn't get enough air. I found out later from my mother that it was at that precise moment that Ronnie went into a seizure. My parents were driving him up to Sloan-Kettering for a checkup when it happened.

They rushed him in and found out that his cancer had spread to his lungs, his brain, his whole body. It was like I had some visceral connection with my brother. That's what they say about identical twins when they feel each other's pain, but you don't have to be physically related to your sibling to feel that level of closeness.

We didn't have much time left. Ronnie knew it was over, but he didn't want my parents to see the unbearable pain he was in. One night, toward the end, he asked me to sit by his bed, hold his hand, and help him through it. It was just the two of us together again, like when we were little kids, facing the fear of what was ahead.

My brother died in May 1984. I felt paralyzed with a sadness so profound, there are no words to describe it. The three of us he left behind clung to one another for dear life. The tears just kept coming. Not long after the funeral, I had a dream. Ronnie's room was in the attic, and I was trying to get up a small set of stairs that led to a hole. I struggled to get through, and when I got to the other side, my brother Ronnie was there, apparently alive. He was playing poker with two other kids, and he looked up from his cards, irate. "*What are you doing here?*" he asked me. "*You have no business being here. You can't see me now. You have to go back. This is not your time!*"

I told my mother about the dream the next morning, and her eyes grew wide with shock. There was no way I could have known this, because I was never on these trips to the hospital with them, but according to the description I gave her, those two boys were the kids Ronnie used to play poker with when they were all waiting for chemo. They both died before Ronnie did. I never met them, but Mom couldn't believe how accurate my description was.

I feel a spiritual connection to the family that raised me. I had the kind of relationship with my adoptive brother that comes from being in a tight-knit clan. We were both just trying to

survive in the crazy Italian family we were placed in. We were surrounded by all these loud, boisterous, funny people. We were
observers of the madness. Ronnie was my childhood. We could
be ourselves with each other. My definition of family is that you
can be at your absolute worst with them and they will still
love you. They will communicate with total honesty. You don't
have to put up a facade. We know one another so well not because we share DNA but because we share a history. I just don't
have that kind of relationship with my sisters, and it's come to
the point where I have to accept that maybe I never will.

BEST-CASE SCENARIO

But reunited siblings *can* make their own history together. It's
possible to create a new kind of family dynamic when everyone
keeps an open heart. I've seen long-lost brothers and sisters accept each other from the moment they first meet. For whatever
reason, both people have made the decision to find a place for
each other in their lives.

Joani O'Brien wasn't looking for her sisters when she called
me. She had no idea they existed. She was like 98 percent of all
my clients, seeking to answer lifelong questions about her birth
mother. Joani knew she had been adopted since she was seven
years old. Her parents were open about it. They'd also adopted
her brother, and they were willing to share whatever they knew
about their children's origins, which was little. All Joani knew
was that she'd been born April Ann Anderson on January 27,
1964, at Meadowbrook Hospital on Long Island, New York.

Her search was the usual stop-and-start effort that happens when you hit obstacle after obstacle. She had one lucky
break when she wrote to the hospital to ask for her medical
records at the time of her birth. They accidentally included the
medical chart of her birth mother, along with her name, Cheryl

Anderson, and her address at the time she gave birth. When Joani contacted me with the information she already had, I knew I could solve the case in a matter of days. But what I learned wasn't good news. Her birth mother's life had been cut short by breast cancer when she was thirty-seven.

When I told Joani, she was devastated, although in her heart of hearts, she'd had a feeling her birth mother was already gone. But there was something else I could share with her that might offset the sense of loss: She had three sisters. Cheryl, Joani's mom, had given birth not long after she graduated from high school, when she was just nineteen. As far as we can tell, Cheryl moved away and took an apartment by herself so that her family would know nothing about the birth. Shortly after giving up Joani for adoption, Cheryl moved by herself to the other side of the country and settled in Ventura, California, where she married not once but three times. Cheryl had Casie, her second daughter, with her second husband. She had Jessica and Lauren with her third husband, Eric. Neither Eric nor Joani's sisters had any idea there was another child.

I gave Joani a few days to process the news; then I gathered the information she needed to get in touch with her siblings. I gave her Eric's number as the main point of contact, and he asked that she hold off over the weekend, until he had a chance to speak with the girls first. He didn't want the phone call to come out of the blue. Of course, she obliged.

Joani had always wanted a sister, but three was overwhelming. These were grown women with lives of their own.

"I was freaking out, thinking, What if they reject me? What if they want nothing to do with me?" Joani recalled.

As it turned out, all three of the sisters were dying to meet her. Joani was prepared for more interrogations, to prove she was legit, but that was the furthest thing from the girls' minds. They were thrilled and excited when they found out they had a big sister. They questioned nothing. They just wanted to get to know her.

NEW BIG SIS

Casie, the eldest of the three, could think of nothing else from the moment her stepfather told her the news on Sunday morning. Her main concern was whether Joani had been raised well, in a loving family. She cared about Joani and embraced her before they even spoke.

"I couldn't bear the thought of a sister of mine living a tumultuous life, in and out of foster homes. I just wanted her to be happy," Casie said. The same thoughts kept running through Casie's mind. *Will she like me? Will I have all the answers she wants? Will she be disappointed?*

By Monday morning, Joani contacted each sister, one by one. She was shaking as she made the first call, only to reach Casie's voice mail. Feeling awkward, she left a message: "Hi, Casie. My name is Joani O'Brien. Oh jeez, how do you leave a message like this? I am your long-lost sister. If you have time, please call me back. I'd love to hear from you."

Six minutes later, Casie was on the phone.

"Hi, Joani, this is your long-lost sister!"

"Which one?"

"Casie!"

They gabbed for the next three and a half hours. The conversation flowed easily. They laughed and they cried. Casie learned that Joani came from a wonderful, stable home, had been happily married to the same man for twenty-one years, and had two beautiful teenage daughters. She'd spent her whole life in California, living in the Bay Area, just six hours away from where Casie and her sisters had grown up in Ventura. Joani learned that Casie shared the same quick wit and they both were social butterflies.

The long conversation was repeated two more times. Each sister was overjoyed to hear from Joani. Lauren e-mailed Joani photographs of herself and her family, and each discovered odd coincidences about the other. They share the same features and mannerisms and are both very active and health-conscious. Coincidentally, at the age of sixteen, they both even held a first job at Baskin-Robbins.

"I was so pleased to discover that talking to Joani came with such ease," said Lauren. "It was as if we had known each other for years. I genuinely loved her and felt close to her from that first conversation."

After speaking with Jessica, Joani immediately realized they shared the same silliness and carefree attitude, though both women were also driven and ambitious. Joani learned that her mother died when the girls were very young: Casie was six, Jessica four, and Lauren three. They told her what little they could about their mother—that she was tough, cheerful, and never let anyone see when she was feeling down. She was always impeccably put together. She worked as a manicurist at a local salon. She was heavily involved in the community through her church and was president of the Police Wives' Association, but no one really got that close to her.

"People who knew my mom always said they felt like she was holding something back," remarked Casie.

What she didn't hold back was her affection for her girls. Cheryl refused to let them see her suffer from her illness. If anything, she was in denial that the cancer would kill her. She didn't want to believe that she could be taken away from her daughters so soon. When it happened, the girls were blindsided. They had no idea she was that sick, and Eric never really spoke about it afterward.

A PIECE OF HER

Joani now feels protective of all three of her younger sisters. She knows that if her mother had kept her, she would have ended up raising them. There are times Casie wishes she had.

"Seeing Joani for the first time was like getting a little piece of my mom back," said Casie, choking back tears. "She completes us."

Today, all four of the sisters are discovering a little bit of their mother in one another. Joan and Lauren, the youngest, look most like Cheryl and share the same headstrong, resilient personality. Jessica, who is a hairdresser and makeup artist in Hollywood, has her mom's artistic touch, and Casie has her sense of humor and way with words. All of the sisters are obsessive list makers. Every day, they have to write down the things they need to do, then check off the list. Casie feels certain their mother would have wanted them to be together, supporting one another as grown women.

All three of Joani's sisters made it clear to her that they didn't want this reunion to be just a onetime phone call. They wanted a full-on relationship, with regular get-togethers. They wanted to celebrate holidays and major family events together. Joanie was signing on to be a full-fledged member of the family. She made the effort to fly out and meet each sister and her family. First, she visited Jessica in Los Angeles, where Joani was taken to see the house where the girls had grown up. Jessica shared what few photos and memories she had. Jessica also took her to the grave site where their mom was buried. They brought four roses, one for each sister, and placed them on her grave.

Joani continued her travels, visiting Lauren in Utah and Casie in Michigan, and each trip made her more excited for the next. Today, they see one another several times a year and speak on the phone at least once a week. They're building their own family history together and creating new memories. They're not bitter that their mother never revealed her secret. They're convinced that if she had known she really was dying, she would have written a letter to tell them. But they're just grateful Joani found them. They can't imagine their lives without one another.

"To think I could have gone through my whole life not knowing I had these three sisters," Joani said.

It was the best possible reunion—beyond anything I could have hoped for these four amazing woman. Two years later, Casie called me because she wanted to thank me personally for helping the sisters reunite. Coincidentally, I heard from her just as I was trying to figure out the perfect case to include in a chapter about siblings. I've seen many successful reunions between brothers and sisters over the years, but this one goes from strength to strength. Casie sent me a copy of a letter the three sisters had written to Joani for her forty-seventh birthday. They sent it to her, along with a scrapbook of memories and photos of their mother and themselves, to catch Joani up on the childhood she had missed with them. Their love and appreciation of one another moved me to tears.

January 15, 2011

Dear Joan, Joani, Jo:

The three of us decided that we wanted to write you a letter expressing just how special you are to us. We wanted to give you a very meaningful gift for your birthday—a scrapbook of as many pictures and memories that we could gather, all in one place—for you. We know that it has taken many years for you to gain answers to many questions that you have had throughout your life, and we feel that it is owed to you to have a special book all to yourself. We know that it will mean a lot to you and be a priceless gift. It is the least we could do, being that you gave us a tremendous gift—you!

We remember clearly the day that our father told us that you existed. Our hearts skipped a beat, tears welled in our eyes, and excitement fluttered in our stomachs. We were full of emotions. There wasn't a single moment that any of us even entertained the idea of not making contact with you.

We were confused and thrilled. Surprised and elated. We hurried off the phone, called each other and cried, and then told our significant others the good news. We remember exactly where we were and what we were doing at the time. We look back often, reminiscing over how this has all come about—reminding us just how fortunate we truly are.

Learning that you had two beautiful daughters and a devoted, supportive husband only added to the happiness we felt. We felt so privileged to have become aunts and sisters-in-law again!

Joani, you have been such a blessing in our lives. You are so genuinely kind and attentive. You show so much interest and effort in staying connected with us. We love your sense of humor. We love that we can pick up the phone and talk for hours if we wanted to. We love that you value family. You show integrity, empathy, and strength when those you love and those that love you need it the most. You are stunningly beautiful inside and out. When we grow up we want to be just like you!

We never could have imagined that gaining a sister would be so natural and so easy. We didn't know what to expect. We hoped for the best-case scenario with you and our hopes were more than fulfilled. The instant connection with you was a true testament that you were ours—our big (little) sis. We look forward to so many years of making up for lost time. We look forward to building our relationships as sisters, and as families. We thank you and Pamela Slaton for finding us. We thank God and Mom for creating you so that we could be reunited. We love you with all our hearts.

Love,
Your Sisters

The Lesson: It Takes Work

If anything, a reunion is easier with siblings, but it still takes work.

By definition, a brother or sister is someone with whom you have shared your childhood; knowing anyone is something that you do day by day. You don't share a background and history with siblings who were given up. Whatever bond you do have comes from the shared oddities of your DNA and the commonalities of family connected by blood. But that's not the same as living in the same home and sharing experiences within the family that raises you.

The sisters in this chapter have amazing relationships with one another, but that is because they have made a conscious effort. They are at places in their lives where they are okay and more than open to being sisters for one another. Joani's siblings wanted to be in this relationship as much as she did. It was a shared commitment. To feel that connection, all parties have to be involved and willing to put in the time and effort.

Even a connection with a sibling, without all the baggage that comes with your birth parents, isn't automatic. Joani's reunion is a best-case scenario, but these women all had good upbringings and shared similar values. How brothers and sisters get along also depends on how supportive the rest of the family is. As saddened as Joani and her sisters were about the passing of their birth mom, maybe the fact that she had been taken out of the equation simplified things. All I know is that I love my sisters, but I am facing up to the fact that my relationship with them can never be like the one Joani has with her younger siblings. And that's okay.

In fact, after writing this book and going back to edit this chapter, I realized that I had some soul-searching to do. I am very hard on the people in my life. I am an adoptee, after all. As I write this, my sister Kathy and her family, along with my own, will be heading out in a week to go on vacation in Lake George, New York, which has become somewhat of a family ritual. I realize that this is my family and that I do genuinely love them all. I know that I have had a major wall up around me, and I have promised myself to be less guarded and accept people for who they are. I just need to love them even when I feel they are not measuring up to my standards of what I expect from people. I am fiercely loyal and have a tendency to put other people's needs before my own. If this is the way that I choose to live, I have no right to demand that of others. I know that this coming vacation is just what we all need—both families together, laughing and just being our silly selves.

CHAPTER TEN

Never Too Late

• • •

She was a petite blond bombshell from Pennsylvania Dutch country, and she was about to get married. The thirty-one-year old divorcée was never single for long—she was like catnip to men. But apparently, that wasn't enough. On the eve of her wedding, she learned that her fiancé was cheating on her, so she called it off. There was just one problem: She was pregnant.

When she found out, a few weeks after the nuptials were supposed to have happened, she told her fiancé that she would reconsider marrying him if she delivered a healthy baby. She wanted to keep the child, even if it meant staying with a philanderer. The pregnancy went smoothly, and when the time came, her best girlfriend took her to St. Vincent's Catholic Hospital in Philadelphia. She had a girl, and the baby looked just like her. For two days, she nursed and cuddled the infant. She was perfect. She had all ten fingers and toes and a full thatch of honey-colored hair. By the second day, she was looking forward to presenting the child to her former fiancé—the baby's father. She couldn't wait to take her home and start her little family, even if it wasn't the most perfect beginning. But she never saw her baby again.

RANDOM CHAT

Fast-forward fifty-one years. We live in South New Jersey, not too far from Pennsylvania, and my husband, Mike, makes a living as an independent contractor, doing painting and construction jobs on homes across the region. He was painting the home of Maureen Donahue one day in 2002 when the two got to talking. Mike is a friendly, chatty kind of guy and he's always talking me up to anyone who'll listen. I'm lucky to have a partner who's so supportive of what I do. He's my best PR guy. When the subject of adoption came up, he told Maureen about all my success stories, and my own experience finding my mother, and then he gave her my number. She was intrigued. Maureen was adopted and she'd tried and failed to find her birth mother several times. She'd long since given up, but her conversation with my husband got her thinking again.

Maureen's parents, who'd adopted her in 1951, were open with her about her adoption as far back as she can remember. That attitude was unusual for those days. Her parents told her that her adoptive mother couldn't have her own children because she was past childbearing years, so they went to a Catholic Charities agency to pick out a baby. They went up and down the aisles, looking at infants in their cots, but none of the babies seemed like the child that was right for them. They were about to give up, when they saw a crib tucked behind the door. In it was Maureen. They knew immediately that she was the one, so they took her home. Her birth mother had been too young and too poor to keep her, which was their good fortune. It was a sweet tale but probably one Maureen's parents embellished a bit to protect her from the sense of stigma commonly attached to adoptees in those days. "I knew it was just a story they made up to make me feel good," Maureen admitted.

THE CHOSEN ONE

Maureen's mother, a homemaker, used to tell her that if kids in school ever picked on her for being adopted, she should tell them she was chosen and that their parents were stuck with what they got.

"I used that line a few times," Maureen said.

Maureen has no complaints about her upbringing. She was a navy brat who spent her childhood wherever her father, an active naval officer, was posted—at Guantánamo Bay, in Cuba, and later in Sanford, Florida. She was extremely close to her family. An only child, she was precious to them, and they were very protective of her. When her father retired, the family moved back to Philadelphia, where Maureen's mother's family was from. They moved into a row house where Maureen's maternal uncle and grandmother were living, and the family of three grew into five. She effectively had two sets of parents.

But Maureen often chafed against all the rules of the people who cared for her. They were from an older generation, and she was coming of age in the sixties. As a teenager, Maureen got pretty good at sneaking off with her friends to go drinking and partying. Even when she was at college studying nursing, she had to abide by an eleven o'clock curfew.

"If my parents had known what I was up to, they'd have killed me," Maureen said.

FIRST STEPS

Maureen was also growing increasingly curious about her birth mother. She didn't dare share this fact with her parents. She knew it would hurt them, especially her mother, who was afraid she'd run away to try to find her birth mother whenever they had a fight. On the sly, she started asking questions about her adoption in high school, but the nuns told her she shouldn't look, and that she should be happy with what she had. No one could give her any direction. But in college, friends were talking about the fact that Pennsylvania had opened up the records for preadoption birth certificates. Maureen wasted no time and wrote to the state offices in Harrisburg. The father's name was listed as "unknown." But she found out her birth mother's name (I will call her Deidre Lutz) and was shocked to learn that she'd been all of thirty-one when she gave her child up for adoption. All her life, Maureen had assumed her birth mother was a teenager and therefore too young to keep her. It just didn't make any sense.

Maureen's parents had already told her that she'd been born at St. Vincent's in Philadelphia and that her mother had been in a home for unwed mothers. Maureen's cousin, who had also been adopted, had already found her birth mother by writing to the Catholic diocese in Philly, so Maureen did the same. A nun confirmed where she'd been born and told her that the home had burned to the ground, along with all the birth and adoption records. That was a blow, but she was able to tell Maureen that her mother had come in with a man who identified himself as the baby's uncle.

STONES UNTURNED

Over the years, Maureen's attempts at a search didn't get much further. She looked in the White Pages of her birth mother's hometown in Pennsylvania but had found no one with the name she'd been given. She saw a television show about adoption searches and got the idea she should find out who had a driver's license with the name Deidre Lutz. She wrote to the state, which sent back a long list, and Maureen wrote to every one of them. She didn't disclose that she was adopted and look-ing for her birth mother. Instead, she spun a story about how she was looking for an old school friend of her mother's. That would at least narrow down which of the Deidres was the right age to be her birth mother. Of the forty or fifty people Maureen wrote to, most wrote back. About half of the respondents said they wished they were the right person.

That was in the 1970s, before it was possible to do a quick Internet search. When Maureen's father discovered what she was up to, he asked her please not to tell her mother, so she shelved the search. After her mother passed away in 1977, Mau-reen stepped up her efforts, writing to Sally Jesse Raphael and Oprah for help. That led nowhere. The hosts of these shows got thousands of requests like Maureen's. Eventually, she let it go. At best, she figured, all she'd learn would be her family's medical history. If Deidre had given birth to Maureen at age thirty-one, it was a long shot that her birth mother would still be alive.

Maureen's encounter with Mike got her thinking again. The timing was better, because both of her parents had passed away. Maureen never stopped wondering what could prompt a fully grown woman to give up her child, especially now that Maureen had three kids of her own. She wasn't upset about it, because she'd had a good life, but it was the big unanswered question. She took another two years to mull it over, and fi-nally, in December 2004, her husband asked her what she wanted for Christmas. "I want to find my mom," she told him.

Maureen sent me all her records. After her father died, she found a copy of her adoption record, which showed the adop-tion hadn't been finalized until 1953. She had all the court documents, signed by the judge, her original birth certificate, and some of the information vaguely recollected by the St. Vincent nuns. It was a better start than most. Within two days, I'd found Deidre. She was eighty-six and still in good health. She'd been married three times, and Lutz was her first married name, so it's no wonder Maureen hadn't been able to locate her birth mother on her own.

CRITICAL MOMENT

Suddenly, it was real. Maureen didn't know what to do. I think she'd been expecting me to fail, and the reality that she could now be reunited with her birth mother freaked her out, to say the least. Maureen came over to my house in Jersey and I gave her all the information. I told her everything she needed to know about what can happen with a reunion. It can be disappointing and painful, but it usually goes well. Good or bad, it offers answers, and most adoptees never regret the decision to search. Either way, I said, she should be prepared.

"So what do I do now?" she asked me.

"You call."

"I need to think about it."

Maureen got up, took her file, and was about to walk out the door, when she stopped, turned around, and said, "No, let's do this. Can you call for me? If I don't do it now, I never will."

She came back into my office and sat down as I picked up the phone to dial. On the third ring, Deidre answered.

"Hello, Deidre?" I said.

"Yes. Who is this?"

"My name is Pamela Slaton. Is it okay for you to talk?"

Deidre excused herself and went to turn down the television. I wanted to make sure there were no other family members around who might be listening in on the conversation. But she was alone.

"How can I help you?" she asked.

"Well, I am hoping you can help me. I am doing genealogy research for someone who was born on December 4, 1951. Her name at birth was Mary Lutz, but she was raised with the name of Maureen Philips." (The nuns sometimes named the babies Mary or Joseph for obvious reasons.)

"I did have a daughter, dear, but she died. That's what they told me at the hospital."

"Oh my gosh, Deidre, I don't know how to tell you this. I am not sure you were told the truth. The person I am helping was adopted and was born on the same date your daughter was born."

I paused, giving her a moment to take it all in, then said, "Are you okay, Deidre?" There was a long silence on the other end of the phone. I was afraid she'd fainted.

"Deidre, I don't know how to tell you this, but your daughter is sitting right here with me. She did not die."

Deidre choked back a sob and said, "Oh my God. Does she want to talk to me?"

"Of course she does!"

The two women got on the phone. The conversation was stilted. These are always tense conversations and the fear of rejection is palpable. How do you ask a complete stranger some of the most intimate and emotional questions that you are burning to ask?

But that wasn't the case. Maureen was never given up. Deidre told her she thought she was dead. After the second day in the hospital, the nurses came to her and told her that her baby girl had died. Deidre asked what funeral arrangements needed to be made, and whether she could see her daughter, but she was told that would not be possible. They explained that there were tests to be done because Maureen was a forceps baby. It sounded fishy, but Deidre trusted what she was told. After all, it was a nun who gave her the information. As painful as it was to learn her baby had passed away, she decided she would just have to get on with her life. Now, with the phone call, her daughter had come back to life, fifty-five years later.

I later learned that Deidre had carried a picture of her infant daughter in her wallet that whole time.

THE COVER-UP

Piecing it all together, we figured out that the "uncle" who had shown up at the hospital was none other than Deidre's former fiancé. However, Deidre had been unaware of his visit because he never came into her hospital room to see her. But apparently, Maureen's father wanted nothing to do with an illegitimate child, so he went to the hospital to arrange for her to be put up for adoption. It wasn't legal to take a child away from the mother without her knowledge, but back then it was such a scandal to have a child out of wedlock that it wasn't unknown to enlist nuns or hospital officials to sweep the whole scandal under the carpet, all in the name of "doing the right thing."

Deidre was a Mennonite, but not the kind who wore the white bonnets. She was a member of a more liberal branch of the sect, which permitted modern clothing and, apparently, divorce. But Maureen's birth father came from a strict Mennonite family. A child born out of wedlock would not have been accepted by his people. I don't know what he told Deidre when she said she'd marry him if she gave birth to a healthy baby, but he clearly had no intention of being a father to his child. Instead, to protect his reputation and preserve his freedom to pursue other women, he betrayed Deidre and Maureen and broke their mother-daughter bond with a cruel lie.

STOLEN MOTHERHOOD

Deidre's immediate family had known she was pregnant, and they found the story of sudden death strange. But Deidre was left with no choice but to work though her grief and figure out a way to survive. She worked most of her life as a waitress in a small-town diner and didn't retire until she was seventy-nine.

Deidre married again a few years after Maureen was born, but she couldn't have any more children. She ached to be a mother again, but her second husband died young, and by the time she married her third, that part of her life was over.

Maureen learned all this in dribs and drabs as the two women got to know each other. On December 22, just in time for Maureen to get her Christmas wish, they made their first date for lunch at a favorite diner near the assisted-living facility where Deidre was now residing. Maureen didn't want to upset Deidre by grilling her too hard. She also sensed a little suspicion on Deidre's part. It took a little while for her to believe that her long-lost daughter really was alive. They'd missed a lot of years and there was so much catching up to do, but it couldn't be forced.

TWO REBELS

In the five years since their reunion, Deidre and Maureen have made a point of meeting every two or three weeks for breakfast, and they chat at least once a week over the phone. The time they spend together revolves around the Mennonite-run seniors' apartment building in Pennsylvania where Deidre's two sisters also live with their husbands. Sometimes mother and daughter take a drive to the nearby nursing home where Deidre's ninety-three-year-old husband, who has Alzheimer's, is spending his last days. Then they grab lunch and run errands on the way back to Deidre's apartment.

Maureen has not been able to find out more details about Deidre's circumstances at the time she thought she'd lost her baby. The timing has never seemed quite right to push for answers, and Maureen no longer feels the need to know. Instead, they have formed a new kind of mother-daughter bond based on friendship. They laugh a lot when they're together, like two kids. They've discovered that there are many parallels in their lives. Both women married three times. In their youth, they were both head-turning blondes. They're both blunt and tell it exactly the way they see it, although they sometimes regret going too far. They like the same sporty, chic style of clothing. They can't eat onions.

Maureen's a take-charge kind of person, and so is Deidre, who is feisty and sharp as a tack. She still drives everywhere, including to the beauty shop where she gets her hair done twice a week. She is meticulous about her appearance and loves to shop. She also maintains a youthful curiosity about the world around her, keeping up with everything that's on the news. She is hip to all that's going on around her, including popular culture. If you ask her a question about the kids on the Jersey shore, Deidre will know the answer. She's no typical ninety-one-year-old.

Both mother and daughter march to the beat of their own drummer. "Rebel" was Maureen's nickname when she was growing up in Florida. Considering her Mennonite background, Deidre's always been quite the free spirit herself. Three marriages, even in her family's more relaxed branch of the Mennonite Church, are unusual. But she has an extremely outgoing personality, which, combined with her knockout looks, was bound to attract a string of suitors. Looking back, Maureen is convinced that if she had been raised by her more permissive and indulgent birth mother, she'd have run wild, and that probably would not have been a good thing.

"I am learning more and more about how much I am like her every time we get together," Maureen told me.

Growing up, Maureen was always drawn to the Pennsylvania Dutch country, with its rolling wooded hills, deep valleys, and lush farmland. This region of southeastern Pennsylvania is where Deidre, and a long line of her ancestors, hailed from. On family vacations to the area, Maureen was inexplicably happy and reveled in the local culture.

MAKING IT FIT

Maureen's gradually gotten to know the family members and friends in her mother's circle. Deidre still hasn't announced Maureen's existence to all her former coworkers, and it took a year before she mustered up the courage to invite Maureen to a family reunion. Even though it was long ago and times have changed, there's still some lingering embarrassment over the fact that she had a child out of wedlock. Deidre's a proud woman and she doesn't want to have to explain herself. But Maureen has been introduced to all the most important people in her mother's life, including Deidre's sisters, cousin, cousin's daughter, and a young woman named Ruth—a former colleague at the diner where she worked—whom Deidre refers to as her "adopted" daughter.

Deidre had a tendency to take young women under her wing. She was extremely close to her two nieces and spoiled them rotten. They were all surrogates for Maureen. The fact that she could never have a child again upset Deidre more than she cared to admit. She recently confessed that December 4, Maureen's birthday, was always a sad day for her. She never got over the loss.

Maureen, in turn, has gone all out to integrate Deidre into her life. Deidre has met Maureen's husband and her three grown sons. She attended her middle grandson's wedding, and visits their summer home in Long Beach, New Jersey, every year to hang out with the family. The boys were very protective of their mother at first and a little skeptical of Deidre's past, but they've grown to love Deidre and now they call her "Grandma." At first, Maureen asked Deidre what she wanted to be called. "You can call me Deidre, Didi, or Mom. Whatever you like, dear," her mother told her.

But since Deidre started sending her cards that say "To My

Daughter," Maureen has taken to calling her birth mother "Mom." It's finally starting to feel comfortable to think of her that way, although it's not a conventional mother-daughter relationship.

"It's kind of hard to find the right card for the birth mother who didn't raise you," Maureen explained.

But she considers the time they spend together extremely precious. She's grateful for every day she has with her birth mother, and they never hang up the phone without saying "I love you." Deidre's healthy, but there's no telling how much longer she has. There are moments when Maureen wishes she'd found her birth mother sooner, but she's glad it didn't happen while her adoptive mother was still alive. Maureen was only twenty-five when her mother died. They'd drifted apart when Maureen was a teenager, but they started getting closer in 1974, when Maureen's first son was born and she began to identify more with her mother's overprotective nature.

Getting to know her birth mother now that she is a mother and grandmother is helping Maureen appreciate what motherhood is all about. It's helped her to understand many of the things she's done in her life, and why. Having a mother back in her life after losing her adoptive mother so young has been a godsend. At this late stage, she and her birth mother understand each other on many levels. There's a richness to their relationship that comes with wisdom and life experience. Their connection may not be easy to define in conventional terms, but it's profound.

"To have a mother back in my life at this age means so much. I don't know why it took this long, but it happened for a reason," Maureen told me.

The Lesson: You're Never Too Old for a Mother

I believe that you always need a mother, no matter how old you are. I am keenly aware of that now.

Maureen was not counting on finding her birth mother alive. She was ambivalent about pursuing the search because she assumed that the woman who had given birth to her would be dead by now. But she still needed that closure. It's never too late to get the answers you need.

That maternal connection will always matter. Maureen is a grandmother, with grown children, but that means that her relationship with her birth mother can be that much richer. The two women can relate to each other on a whole different level. Maureen lost her adoptive mother when she was still a young woman. But this new maternal bond can fill a void. They can share their children, their insights, their wisdom, and their love.

Thank God she didn't turn around and walk away from my office that day. Maureen and Deidre's story shows that God has a plan. It takes courage to go forward, but the rewards can be unbelievable. So many clients say to me, "Oh, it's too late. I shouldn't bother." But you may be surprised by what you find. If you take that attitude, you could be missing out on the opportunity of a lifetime.

CHAPTER ELEVEN

Mistaken Identity

• • •

The scene played out in young Ann Haralambie's head a thousand times before: Her birth mother, a beautiful Irish Catholic girl, lay sleeping while the fire around her raged out of control. Ann, the infant, was crying in a bassinet in the next room. Her father was just coming home from a late shift at work when he saw what was happening and rushed in to grab the baby, wrap her in a blanket, and take her out onto the street to safety. Then he ran in to save his beloved wife, but by then it was too late. The whole place was engulfed in flames. He was so distraught by her loss that he put baby Ann up for adoption.

Of course, this was pure make-believe—just one of several stories that weaved tragic circumstances around the story of Ann's adoption. As a child, Ann could only imagine her birth parents as upstanding married Catholic people and, whether she'd died in childbirth or drowned at sea, her mother always wound up dead.

"I must have watched too many Shirley Temple movies, because I couldn't imagine it any other way," Ann explained.

Not that Ann needed to create some alternative fantasy to escape the fate of being a miserable orphan. Her upbringing as an adoptee was as good as it gets. She and her family lived in a comfortable middle-class home in Larchmont, New York. Her father was a pediatrician and her mother was a nurse, but she retired to become a full-time homemaker when she and her husband started their family. They were supportive and loving, and totally open about the fact that their children were adopted.

"I'm sure my parents would be horrified if they knew how much I was thinking about all this," Ann admitted.

But she did obsess, for as long as she can remember. Ann's earliest memory is of being told by her adoptive mother that she had another mother out there. She was a little over two years old, and still in nursery school. Everything about that conversation is still vivid in her mind. Per usual for the toddler, she trailed behind her mom like a little limpet while she did the laundry. One day, when Mrs. Haralambie was finished with the ironing and folding, she led Ann upstairs to her brother's bedroom and set the wicker laundry basket down at the foot of the bed. Then she picked up her daughter, propped her up on some pillows, and sat Ann down next to her.

"Ann, honey, I have something I need to tell you," she said.

"What, Mommy?"

"You have another mommy somewhere, and you're not able to be with her. But I am still your mother. Your mommy and daddy love you very much."

LIFELONG OBSESSION

By the time Ann was in elementary school, she was actively thinking about finding her birth parents. More specifically, she thought about finding her father, as she figured there was no way her mother could possibly be alive. She assumed she never would have been given up unless some tragedy had happened. That's how it was in the movies.

As she got older, she began to realize that probably wasn't the case, knowing a thing or two about teenage pregnancies and what could go wrong. She figured her mother was just a regular girl who found herself in trouble, and that shifted her focus in trying to find her. This was the 1970s, before the adoption search movement had begun, but it occurred to Ann she might be able to track down her original birth certificate. She couldn't, of course, because information about New York State adoptions was kept under lock and key.

By her early twenties, when she was just starting law school, Ann heard there were other ways to search. She started by going to the Children's Aid Society offices in Manhattan to ask for non-identifying information. The people there weren't exactly helpful. They wouldn't even tell her where the receiving home was—the agency in Brooklyn where she stayed before she was adopted. All she learned was that when her unmarried birth mother was pregnant, she had been sent to New York to stay with friends of the family. I only later found out that the birth mother went to Queens to live with her older sister, who was also pregnant at the time, but married. They told her that her birth mother was "from the East, but not New England, and not the Deep South." The woman in charge of Ann's case sat behind her desk, muttering under her breath about what she could or could not reveal. It was driving Ann crazy.

"I swear if I hadn't had to pass through a maze of offices there and back, I would have snatched that file from her hands and taken off with it!" she recalled.

PUTTING TOGETHER THE PIECES

Ann took careful notes and tried to piece together what little information she had. Her adoptive mother happened to remember that when she'd picked Ann up from the agency and filled out the paperwork, someone on the staff remarked, "Oh, I see you kept the baby's name as Ann. Her mother's name was Ann."

Ann's adoptive parents also gave her an adoption decree.

According to that document, her name at birth had been Ann Nicholson. She made the leap that her mother would also have been Ann Nicholson, since illegitimate children traditionally take on their mothers' surname. That information, combined with the detail that her mother came from a prominent family, went to college, and belonged to a sorority, led Ann to conclude that her birth mother might be found in *Who's Who Among Students*. Now at work on her third degree at the University of Arizona, Ann spent hours of her free time scouring the pages of that book, hoping to come across an Ann Nicholson who might fit the profile.

The search file Ann had started was growing thick, but she was still no closer to finding her birth mother. Then something happened that she was sure would lead to a big break in the case. At one point, she became so debilitated with an undiagnosed joint disease that she was wheelchair-bound for two weeks. Despite the pain, Ann was thrilled. She figured she now had solid grounds for petitioning the court to unseal her birth records for medical reasons. It was her right to contact her birth family to learn about their medical history, and what may be causing her chronic pain.

"I was at my worst, but I considered the illness to be a great gift," she recalled.

BLIND ALLEYS

Her parents petitioned the court on Ann's behalf, but the New York State authorities wouldn't budge. Frustrated at every turn, Ann kept looking. She'd amassed boxes of files. She'd even made charts. She finally narrowed the field down to one possible candidate, a nurse who'd been studying at a Catholic college in New Jersey at the time her mother would have become pregnant. As far as Ann was concerned, all that legwork and deductive reasoning had to be right. Adding to her certainty was her adoptive father's revelation he had bumped into a fellow pediatrician who worked for an adoption agency (the New York medical community was a small enough world at the time for this to happen). Ann's adoptive father mentioned he was interested in adopting a child, and this doctor told him about a baby girl with a good family on both sides, people who were smart and healthy. It made sense that the Ann Nicholson who had been a student nurse would have crossed the bridge from New Jersey to Brooklyn to give birth. She even had two older sisters. Everything seemed to line up.

VIRGIN BIRTH

By now, it was 1978. Ann had launched a flourishing career as a family-law practitioner who specialized in children's rights. Her own pursuit had prepared her well. Her search skills had become so finely honed that she applied them on behalf of her clients, and successfully reunited several adoptees with their birth families. But her own reunion still hadn't happened. Figuring she'd been patient long enough, she found a pretext to visit this Ann Nicholson, whom she'd finally located in New Jersey. She drove there from New York with her best friend.

The Ann Nicholson who greeted her was gracious and kind. But there was one problem. Ann's birth mother's height was listed as five three, and this lady was five seven. However, Ann would not give up. She assumed her birth mother must be one of this woman's sisters. One, also a nurse, was five one. The other, a nun, was five three. It *had* to be the nun, Ann figured.

I've got to hand it to Ann; she is persistent. Years later, a lawyer colleague of Ann's happened to be in Texas for a conference. Ann knew that was where the Nicholson nun worked as a hospital administrator so she asked her friend to stop by and check her out. By then Ann had convinced herself that this was her mother. This particular Nicholson sister was a charismatic Catholic—open-minded and highly spiritual. The only snag was that Sister Mary Jude was a virgin.

Over the next several years, Ann continued her correspondence with the Nicholson sisters. All three agreed to submit to DNA testing. They were sympathetic and wanted to help. Oddly, the two Anns matched on seven out of ten DNA markers, and the other sisters matched on six markers. Any two random people might have two or three matches, but six or seven was unusual. Ann had never seen a case where there were so many matches. The DNA testing ruled out a maternal connection, but Ann suspected there might still be a match somewhere among the Nicholson sisters' extended family. She got to know their cousins, aunts, and uncles, but the hunt still came up cold.

"I figured I had the right church, but the wrong pew," Ann said.

THE BUDDY SYSTEM

Meanwhile, Ann had become deeply involved in the adoption search movement. She'd joined ALMA, the Adoption Liberty Movement Association. She became an unnamed member in a class-action lawsuit undertaken to get New York State to unseal adoption records. ALMA pairs up its members with "buddies" who exchange information and support in their adoption searches, and one of Ann's buddies just happened to be a client of mine. I had found this woman's mother in Arizona within two weeks, so she was impressed enough to pass my name and contact information on to Ann. (A lot of my business comes through referrals.)

Ann's considerable search skills, and the efforts of professional investigators, had yielded nothing. Two years earlier, Ann had had one of those eerie flashes of intuition. She woke up with a sense of urgency that was physical. She felt in her bones that her birth mother must be close to death. Because she sensed it was already too late, she didn't believe I could help her. But with my no find, no fee policy, she decided she had nothing to lose.

When Ann finally called me, I could hear in her voice that she'd lost all hope.

"You don't sound too happy," I told her. "I hope I can change that."

"It's nothing personal. I've done all the obvious things and I just don't see how you'll do any better."

"Listen, Ann," I said. "New York is my backyard. I've done a lot of successful searches for clients with a lot less information than you have. Don't give up yet. You never know."

"I appreciate that, Pam. I guess it's the fact that I've been at this so many years. And this is November, the month I was born. I always get depressed around my birthday."

"I understand. I really do. But maybe we can change that. Send me what you have, and I'll get started."

FRESH EYES

She sent me a huge box with all her research and the findings of the private investigators who had worked on her case. The documents stacked up to the size of three New York City Yellow Pages—the fruits of a lifelong obsession. There were a few clues, but a lot of the information just led you around in circles. Something was wrong, and I literally needed to step outside what was in that box to see it. There was a piece that was either missing or wrong and was throwing off the investigation. But when I ran some of the data, I had a small breakthrough. I narrowed down the mother's state of birth to West Virginia and the birth date to within two or three days. I also found out that her baptismal records in the Archdiocese of New York listed her as Ann Nichols, which was one of three aliases she used, including the name Mary Ann Nicholson. I figured that must be why it had been so hard to find her.

Ann promptly researched all the counties in West Virginia that had a lot of Catholics and Irish immigrants, as well as the communities where there were colleges and universities. She wrote asking for every Ann, Anne, and Mary Ann with the last name of Nichols or Nicholson born within a four-day period in 1930. There were fifty-five counties, so this meant a lot of e-mails. A couple of weeks later, Ann called me with a progress report. "Nothing! Nothing, nothing, nothing! I just don't get it!" she told me.

"This is ridiculous," I said. "Let's try something radical. Let's run a search without the last name."

Within a few days, on January 16, 2009, I struck gold. Ann's birth mother's name was Ann Cottle, although now she was listed under her married name, Ann Kibble. I had an address and a phone number. I also got the name and address of Ann's aunt—Carolyn—the woman Ann's mother lived with while she was pregnant, and likely the only woman in the family who even knew an illegitimate child existed.

I called Ann and said, "Ann, I found her. She's still alive! Do you want me to call her?"

"Oh my God! Yes! Let's do it right now!"

MUTE CRIES

It wasn't my usual practice, but because Ann was a fellow professional, I decided to make this a conference call and put Ann on mute. I'd already left a voice mail at the aunt's number, saying I was doing genealogical work. With Ann on the other line now, I called her birth mother's number. Ann Kibble's daughter-in-law, Michelle, answered the phone:

"Hello, my name is Pamela Slaton and I'm looking for Ann. Is she available?"

"Sorry, you must have the wrong number."

"Oh, well, the listing I have is for Ann Kibble. Are you sure she doesn't live here?"

"Um, no, she doesn't. She passed away two years ago."

I was mortified. I could only imagine the grief Ann must have been going through at that moment. She may have suspected all along that her mother was dead, but that's different from having confirmation. She told me afterward she was relieved I'd had her on mute, because she was shrieking and sobbing. It wouldn't have been the best of introductions to her birth relatives.

Michelle turned the phone over to Matthew, Ann Kibble's youngest son, who was my client Ann's daughter's age.

"What's this all about?" he asked.

I explained to him that I was a genealogist and that I had reason to believe that his mother was also my client's mother.

"Matt, I want to assure you that my client is a very successful lawyer. She's not looking for anything. She's a respectable person who was adopted and just wants to connect with her birth family."

"Maybe so, but I'm sure you must have the wrong family. There is no way my mother would have had a child out of wedlock."

I gave him all the information we had from the agency and our search. It was so obviously a match. Ann, meanwhile, was e-mailing me as she was listening to the conversation, suggesting that I ask him if he'd wanted to see her picture and résumé. He did. I e-mailed them to him on the spot. But even when he was confronted with all the hard evidence, he still couldn't quite believe it.

"Pam, please e-mail this to my sister, Debbie," he said. "She lives near me, so I'll run over there and we'll look at it together and call you back."

This time, everyone was in on the call: Ann (without the mute button), Matt, and Debbie. Matt and his siblings, aunts, and uncles lived in New York's tristate area. The aunt and uncle lived in New Jersey. A few cousins lived on Long Island. Ann had been looking in the right neighborhoods this whole time.

Matt and Debbie couldn't get over Ann's resemblance to their mother. Their uncle Porter confirmed everything. Matt later reported the conversation back to his newfound sister, Ann. "It's time for the truth to come out," Uncle Porter had said. "Your mother was pregnant in 1951 and she came to live with us. The baby was born that November in Brooklyn Hospital."

FAMILY EFFORT

The long-buried family secret had finally exploded like a time bomb. No one had suspected a thing prior to my call, which was as unexpected as a bolt of lightning from a clear blue sky. And yet the family was more excited than upset by this discovery. The e-mails started flying. Debbie's youngest daughter, Laura, invited Ann to join Facebook so everyone could share pictures and connect more quickly. Everyone was working to put the pieces together, Googling names, and digging up old photos.

There were two different stories about why Ann had been given up for adoption. In the first, Ann's mother was a student, pregnant out of wedlock. She broke up with her college sweetheart shortly after Ann was conceived, and Ann's grandparents said that their daughter could not bring home an illegitimate child. Adoption was the only option.

In the second, more accurate version of the story, giving up the child was the decision of Ann's mother, not her grandparents. Her mother tried to hide the pregnancy as long as she could by wearing a girdle. When she couldn't conceal it any longer, she told her parents. Her father, Ann's grandfather, put his arms around her and said, "You can bring the baby home. We'll raise it as our own." But Ann's mother didn't want to face the suspicions of friends and neighbors. Emotionally, it was also easier for her to put the baby up for adoption than to watch her be raised as her baby sister and never be able to claim her as her own.

The truth was hard for Ann to hear, and a far cry from her childhood fantasies. But her uncle Porter told her that her mother never quite got over what had happened. "Your mother thought about you every day," he said. "She was tortured every year on your birthday."

Ann's mother went on to marry and have four other children. She lived a comfortable middle-class life. She never told a soul—not her husband, not even her best friend. At one point, her husband had an affair and they almost divorced, but she got pregnant again, so they stayed together. For her, it was all about keeping up appearances and living a devout life without even a smidgeon of impropriety. But the revelation of her past solved a mystery for her youngest daughter, who became pregnant at sixteen. Ann's mother had been adamant that she not give up the child. "Honey, you have two choices," Anne's mother told her. "Either marry the boy or your father and I will raise your baby here at home."

For such a strict Catholic mother, this was shockingly out of character. Her response was completely inconsistent with everything she stood for. It suggested that Ann's mother didn't want her child to go through the sense of loss she had gone through when she gave up Ann. It was a sign of humanity and vulnerability beneath that flinty, impeccable persona.

As Ann's mother and her husband got older and their kids

started leaving the nest, the husband suggested they adopt. He felt it was only right to provide for a child who needed a family when they had so much to give. But his wife flipped. She was adamant. He couldn't understand why she was so resistant. Their kids figured that to adopt would have felt like the ultimate betrayal. To turn around and adopt when her firstborn had been given up just wouldn't have seemed fair to Ann's mother. The kids were sure their father would never have suggested such a thing if he had known the truth. It was yet another piece of the puzzle of Ann Kibble's life that suddenly fell into place.

THE OTHER HALF

Ann asked if Uncle Porter or Aunt Carolyn had any idea who her father was. Aunt Carolyn, who suffers from mild dementia, piped up in the background: "It was that Rob Williams fella!" (For reasons you will learn, I have changed his name.)

By the time the sun came up, Ann knew where everybody lived, what they did for a living, whom they'd married, and how many kids they had.

"This is overwhelming!" she told me. "After all these years, I never thought I could get so much information so fast!"

Ann decided to find and contact her birth father discreetly. She didn't know what, if anything, he knew, or whether his family had any idea of her existence. The last thing she wanted was to bother him or make him feel uncomfortable. It was easy enough to track him down.

A LAWYER'S DNA

The coincidences were stacking up. Ann's birth father was also a prominent family lawyer in his community, and his two brothers, along with Ann's youngest sister, practiced law. Like Ann, who has a Master's in English and spent a year teaching the subject, her birth father's sister has a Master's in English literature and taught in college. Her mother's sister also has Master's in English, and taught in high school. Her paternal grandfather and great-grandfather had been prominent physicians, like Ann's adoptive father. The parallels between Ann's own life and the lives in her two birth families were extraordinary.

But secrecy was another thing Ann's birth parents had in common. When she called her father, he was stunned to learn of her existence, but he was at least willing to speak with her. He shared information about his medical history and filled her in on the stories of all her family members. He certainly didn't act like a man who was in denial of his paternity. He was even kind. "Like you, I've handled hundreds of adoption cases, and if I was in your place and had been adopted myself, I would feel exactly the same way," he told Ann.

Ann sent him pictures of herself, her daughter, and her grandson, and he was only too happy to receive them. But he asked for some space. His wife was dying, and the last thing he wanted was for her to find out about this on her deathbed.

"I know my birth mother never told you, but didn't you ever expect the knock on the door?" Ann asked him.

"I suppose I knew it was a possibility, but I have an ability to put things out of my mind," he responded.

Ann let it go for a while. She understood his situation completely and did not want to cause his family any further pain. He said he might be ready by the summer. She waited until April, to give everyone time to grieve, and then she reached out to him again.

"Look, Ann, I don't think this is going to work. I don't want my children and grandchildren exposed to this," he said. "I can't meet with you."

"Exposed to what? I'm a respectable person and it's something that happened a long time ago."

"Don't take it personally."

"Are you kidding me? I just want to meet you. The rest of the family doesn't have to know. I'll even meet you somewhere in between so it doesn't have to be the same town. Or I can just show up as another attorney."

"No!"

It was becoming clear he'd never intended to meet her. He'd just been stringing her along for all of these months. Ann was more philosophical than devastated. It was a cold and definitive rejection, but she guessed that her birth father was simply being defensive. Like her birth mother, he found even the semblance of impropriety was unacceptable. This was a proud family man who was an upstanding member of his community. He'd been an Eagle Scout and a marine. He couldn't bear the thought of appearing to have done anything less than what was appropriate.

"Aren't you angry?" I asked her.

"He was raised with the values of truth and honor. This must have been very challenging for him. I'm disappointed, but I understand."

A PLEASANT TWIST

But Ann has cultivated lasting relationships with her siblings and extended family on her mother's side. Mark is her favorite brother. They've since met up in Boston and at Ann's summer home in New Hampshire. Mark attended her daughter's wedding, and they're in regular contact.

"Our values are the same," says Ann.

She's also developed a special fondness for her niece, Laura, who reaches out to Ann on a regular basis for advice. But her closest relationship is with her cousin Casey Hartman—the unexpected reward for Ann's long years of searching. She's convinced the two must have bonded in utero, when her aunt and mother were pregnant four months apart and living under the same roof.

"Casey is my best friend," says Ann. "We talk every day."

Ann is completely at peace with the way she went about her search, and the fact that she got her answers two years too late. Her adoptive parents died long ago, so the timing of her reunion spared them any pain. Even though they wanted her to find her birth family for health reasons, she's certain they would have been hurt by the discovery had they still been alive. Ann is also reconciled to the fact that her birth mother died before she could meet her. It was a secret she was determined to take with her to her grave, and she got her wish.

"God knows better than I did when it was the right time to happen," she told me.

There are still a lot of unanswered questions. And being rejected by her birth father was rough. But Ann's been in this game long enough to know that when you start a search, you have to want to know the truth badly enough to deal with any painful fallout. She wasn't naïve.

"If you aren't willing to go through the devastation of a bad reunion, you don't need to be searching," she maintains.

We've both had our share of ups and downs in our searches, but it was worth it on so many levels. There is nothing to regret. She insists the sadness of not meeting her birth mother in time and the pain of her birth father's rejection were worth it for the relationship Ann now has with her cousin Casey. More important, though, is the relationship she now has with herself.

"I spent my whole life thinking I was the biggest skeleton in my family's closet. I am experiencing a resurrection of my deepest self," she told me.

For now, at least, her birth mother's family accepts her. If anything, her siblings are sorry they missed out on a lifetime of knowing their eldest sister. Ann expects many more ups and downs as she gets to know them and pieces more of her family's history together, but there's tumult in every family. Whatever happens next, what she's found is enough. Her search has given her the greatest gift of all: closure.

"There's a peace now. A physical peace I can feel in my body that I have never felt in my life," she said.

The Lesson: Sometimes You Need a Fresh Pair of Eyes

When you are invested in your search, it's hard to step out of the box. Ann had the skill set to connect with other adoptees easily, but she couldn't step back from her own case. It was only after more than thirty years that she was finally able to let go enough to entrust her search to a third party. I have been a professional searcher for sixteen years, but I hadn't always done this. Even I had to hire a professional searcher to help me.

It's often the case that my clients become obsessive in their search. They finally reach a point where they realize life has to go on and they can't do it anymore. They have to give it over to someone else.

The tragedy was that, after all her efforts, Ann was too late. Her mother was gone. But it might not be a bad thing that she never met the mother who felt such a desperate need to guard her secret. Like I always say, God knows better than we do when the time is right. In the end, Ann's birth family embraced her and made heroic efforts to give her the answers she needed. It was more than enough to bring her closure.

She even got more than she'd hoped to find—a best friend. Her friendship with her cousin was a pleasant surprise twist. But Ann's ability to connect with her extended birth family stems from the fact that she opened herself up to her truth and readily accepted it. She was prepared for any outcome and had no set expectations. That's the key to a successful search. Search for closure and consider anything beyond that a bonus.

CHAPTER TWELVE

Against the Clock

◆ ◆ ◆

W hen you're searching, time isn't always your friend. For many adoptees, it's tempting to wait it out until later in life, when their adoptive parents have passed away, or when they've got the extra cash to invest in professional help. But there are inherent risks. Many of my baby-boomer clients are looking for birth parents who are elderly and frail by now. Some are too late. One of my least favorite things about my job is telling clients that the person they've been waiting their whole lives to meet is no longer alive.

It wasn't that Owen Brown didn't want to find his birth mother. He'd thought about it on and off for most of his fifty-four years. But something held him back from taking that extra step. He didn't want to hurt his adoptive parents, Samuel and Elaine Brown. It was an incredibly close family, with a bond of love stronger than any blood tie. His father, in particular, was an emotional man. Owen still remembers moments of extreme tenderness when he was a toddler. If he cried during the night, his father would get up and crawl into the crib to comfort him.

"I just figured somehow, if he found out I was searching, it would break his heart," Owen told me.

Owen's upbringing was as good as it gets. He had a modest middle-class childhood in a suburban New Jersey home. He had a sister, also adopted, who was four years younger. His parents didn't spoil them, but they were kind, and they taught their kids the importance of giving back to the community through thousands of acts of generosity, large and small. They taught them by example and gave them unconditional love.

"I didn't have a yearning; there was nothing missing from my life," Owen said. "Still, there's always a question in the back of your mind. Who was she?"

THE HIDDEN TRUTH

The business of living his life took over, as it often does for people who are searching. Like most of us, Owen started his search at various points in his life, then stopped. He was half-hearted about it. He had a busy job as an executive on Wall Street, and his family took up the rest of his time. There wasn't much free time to go poring through public records or digging for information he might never find.

But in 2000, at age forty-four, Owen finally did have some free time on his hands. He'd just left a company and had started his own commodities and currencies trading business. He was in the process of setting it up and raising capital, so he spent a lot of time in the office, waiting around. He decided to fill in those extra hours doing a search. He took the step of getting non-identifying details from the agency that had handled his adoption, Louise Wise Services. His parents made no secret of the fact that he was adopted and they never tried to hide his birth name. He learned a few scraps of his birth mother's story and how she came into existence.

Francine was Jewish and the daughter of a barber, born in the first half of 1932. Her parents were good, hardworking immigrants from Poland who just managed to get by. They lived in the Bronx, and when Francine's sister, who was also her best friend, announced she was getting married and moving out of state to New Jersey, Francine was distraught. Back then, getting around wasn't so easy, so the one person she was closest to might as well have been moving to the other side of the country. Francine fled to Florida, hoping that the warm sunshine would help her overcome her sense of loss.

She was twenty-four, naïve, and stunningly beautiful. Tall, with long dark hair, she looked a little like a young Audrey Hepburn. Being on her own and in a rebellious phase of her life made Francine an easy mark for some random playboy. She had a brief affair and the inevitable happened. When she realized she was pregnant, she made her way back home. Her father sent her to a Jewish home for unwed mothers as far away from the Bronx as you could get without leaving the city—Staten Island. This was standard practice in those days. While she was gone, the family's friends and neighbors thought Francine had returned to the old country to visit relatives.

Owen took this very brief bio of his birth mother's life at face value. He understood what she must have gone through. She had done what she thought was best to give him a good life. He didn't blame her. If anything, he was grateful. By the standards of those times, it was the best possible option. But he knew deep down she must have been devastated. All he wanted was to see her, thank her for bearing him, and let her know he'd had a good life with two wonderful parents.

"I'm not trying to sound like Mother Teresa or anything, but I just wanted to do this for her, to give her closure," Owen explained.

I find that many of my adoptee clients feel this way. But Owen is the real deal. Giving back is his life's creed. He even set up a foundation at a small orphanage in Ecuador—Childhood Promise—to help kids get an education and provide them with scholarships. He feels so fortunate in his own life that he wants orphans who didn't get the life he had to feel as if someone truly cares. He doesn't just donate money; he travels down there with his wife and kids at least once a year to visit with these children. He celebrates their birthdays, holidays, and graduations and generally takes the time to talk with them, give hugs, and let them know they matter. He has an especially generous spirit, and he genuinely wanted to do something for his birth mother that could bring her some peace.

A FORTUNATE ERROR

Owen got even closer in his search for his birth mother when he went to the New York Public Library, where all the birth records are kept. He had a hunch that his birth name, Bruce Jacob, would lead him to the truth. He was concerned that his name at birth was just a first and a middle name. But Jacob can also be a Jewish last name. Owen figured there was a chance they had mixed up the middle and last names and that Jacob was, in fact, his family name. It's a rare mistake.

He was right. The name lined up perfectly with the number on his birth certificate. Next, it was a question of pulling out the records for the first half of 1932 to find out his mother's identifying details. Luckily, there were only two girls born before June 30 of that year with the last name Jacob. His mother, Francine, was one of them. But that's where it all fell apart. Francine had long since married and moved away from her family home in the Bronx. Owen decided to shelve his search. He just didn't have the heart to explain to his dad what he'd been up to, so giving up was the easiest option for the time being. His adoptive mother was fine with it. But Samuel Brown had recently suffered a stroke and he was on a lot of medications. Owen figured he was too frail to handle the fact that his son had been looking for his birth mother.

"I knew time was running out and I didn't want to wait forever, but I when I started thinking about my dad's feelings, it just didn't feel right. He'd been there for me my whole life and I didn't want to make him sad," Owen explained.

Ten years later, in 2009, Owen's father passed away. The following year, after recovering from the initial shock and grief of his loss, Owen decided it was time to pick up the trail again. Over the past decade, a lot had changed for adoptees searching for birth parents. There were many more Web sites dedicated to finding birth parents. By July 2010, he'd found someone in California who was part of a certified organization, but when he told her where he was based, she immediately referred him to me. He wasted no time in calling.

"Hi, Pam. I hope you can help me. I was told you have a perfect track record."

"It's not perfect, Owen, but it's pretty darn good. What do you have for me?"

I was impressed with the quality of information Owen had already dug up. Once I have a name, one of my specialties is finding current addresses. I have access to piles of data that can help me track people down.

"This is good, Owen. Leave it to me. I'll get back to you with something within the next three weeks," I told him.

I managed to find her in no time. She had never left the New York area, which always helps. Only her sister and parents knew about Owen. Four years after Owen was born, his mother married and bore a daughter. The husband, Edward, was a vagabond, and he didn't stick around for very long before disappearing for good. Francine was left to raise her little girl on her own. Again, she moved back home to the Bronx, where she had some support from her mother—Owen's biological grandmother. It wasn't much of a life. Francine was lonely. She never married again. She muddled along, but something was always missing.

CLOSE CALL

But it wasn't too late to fill the void. Francine's current address was a nursing home in Fresh Meadows, Queens. That wasn't a good sign. There was no time to waste. I gave Owen the number. He wanted to go there in person and surprise her, but I suggested he call her first. A shock like that might be too much for someone elderly and frail, I cautioned. A phone call gives the person time to mentally prepare for the meeting. But in the end, Owen got his way.

First he called the nursing home's reception desk. They patched him through to her room, but nobody picked up. Owen figured he'd waited fifty-four years, so another day wasn't going to make much of a difference. He called again at the same time the next day. But again, there was no answer. Finally, on the third try, he was put through to the administration office of the nursing home.

"Oh, Mr. Brown. Someone in our office has something to tell you."

Owen's heart sank.

"Is she okay?" he asked.

"I'm afraid I'm not at liberty to say."

Owen felt it would be the ultimate irony if his mother passed away just as he was on the brink of meeting her. It just couldn't be. By now, Owen was frantic. He was having heart palpitations. He wanted this meeting as much for his sake as for hers. Just the chance to make contact one time before she died was all he asked.

The nursing home director called him back. He explained that Francine was in a hospital in Flushing, recovering from a bout of pneumonia. Her overall health had been declining, and she'd been in and out of the hospital a few times over the past three years. Owen wasn't going to take any more chances, so he hightailed it straight to Francine's hospital ward, stopping only to pick up some flowers on the way.

A GLEAM IN HER EYES

When he walked into her room, she was sharing it with another woman of about the same age, but Owen knew immediately which one was his birth mother.

She had a look in her eye. It was probably a look she'd had before, whenever she saw a man who would be about her son's age. It was a look of hope that flashed on her face for a nanosecond, as if she was thinking to herself, *Could this be him?*

Owen walked up to her bed and she smiled.

"These are for you," he said, handing her a bunch of pink roses.

"Who are you?" she asked.

He decided to ease into it. "My name is Owen Brown, and you are Francine. I know a lot about you. My last name used to be Jacob. A long time ago, I was given the name Bruce. I was born on September 11, 1956. Does that ring a bell?"

She looked at him, smiling and nodding. Francine was pretty weak from the pneumonia, but she was alert, and she couldn't stop beaming.

"Francine, I'm your son."

"I know. I just needed to hear you say that. I'd always hoped you'd come and find me, but after all these years, I figured it wasn't going to happen."

Owen sat by her bedside for the next two hours. He didn't know if he would get a chance to see her again. He wasn't sure if she'd pull through. They caught up on each other's lives. They held hands and gazed at each other. Neither of them could stop smiling. Francine told him what he'd already suspected—that she'd never wanted to give him up, but in those days she'd had no choice. As a single mother, she would have been ostracized from her family and society. She told him a little about the family's medical history. She filled him in on his half sister. Some of the details were sketchy, as her memory wasn't perfect, but there was something comfortable and natural about the conversation. He told her she'd made the best decision for him, and then he did what he'd always wanted to do—he thanked her.

"I always knew you had good parents and that you were okay. I had a dream once that you were being held by a woman with a big sweet smile on her face," Francine said.

Nothing Francine told Owen was surprising, but he sensed an inner strength and confidence about her. The conversation continued in fits and starts. She wasn't strong. A couple of times, she faded out and had to close her eyes. But Owen learned a lot about his birth mother during that first visit. He could tell she knew herself. After seventy-eight years, she was set in her ways and opinions. She went through a lot of pain and regret, but it no longer mattered.

"I'm so happy you found me. It always felt like something was missing from my heart and now you've filled it up," she told Owen. "Now I feel complete."

A MENDED HEART

I was dying to hear how the meeting had gone. I was praying it wasn't too late, and hoping to God that Francine was lucid when she finally got to meet her son. I often have this debate with clients about how they should first approach their birth relatives. Showing up out of the blue is always a big no-no. It made me nervous that Owen was going to just turn up at the hospital. But he loved the fact that he could be with her and see the look on her face when he introduced himself to her.

"Obviously, I'm not happy that she was sick and in the hospital, but there was something fortuitous about the way this meeting happened," Owen told me afterward. "There's so much that gets lost in translation when you can't look at someone face-to-face. Her smile spoke volumes."

Thankfully, it wasn't Francine's time to go. She recovered from that bout of pneumonia. Owen's been making a point of trying to see her once a month. The second time he met her, she was in a trauma ward. The hospital was looking for a bed so they could admit her. Her pneumonia was back. He took his son to visit with her, but the conversation was superficial because she could barely speak. Her breathing was labored. The visit lasted only about fifteen minutes. On another occasion, he took the rest of his family to meet her in her room at the assisted-living facility.

He's since learned that from the ages of fifty-two to fifty-seven, she had a live-in male companion whom she never married. Francine's daughter, who was fathered and abandoned by her first husband when she was two, isn't yet ready to meet Owen, and it may never happen. She thought she was an only child and learning of his existence came as a shock.

Through relatives, Owen was informed about the family's medical history, as well as his birth mother's history of melancholy. She was distant and almost never playful, although the one place that gave Francine joy was a family vacation home in Long Beach. He also saw pictures of Francine when she was in her twenties. She was stunning. But there was sadness in her eyes. It was confirmation for Owen that giving him up for adoption cast a shadow over the rest of Francine's life. It made him more determined to keep seeing her.

His adoptive mother would also like to meet Francine when she's well enough. She told Owen, "I want to thank her for giving me the opportunity to raise you."

Meanwhile, Owen doesn't refer to Francine as his mother.

The woman who raised him gets that title. "I don't have any pining in my heart or a need for another mother. But I love the fact that she bore me and gave me up, and that it worked out well. And it gives me great pleasure to see that she's happy now."

There are still a few gaps in Owen and Francine's knowledge of each other. He's hoping she can build up her strength so she can get to know him and his family a little better. He wants to be able to take her out and invite her to his home. But with her frail health, it could all come to an end any day now. Any time they have left is a precious gift.

"I'd love to have more time with Francine. But if nothing else she can go to her grave knowing her son was okay and she did a noble thing. Everything about this feels good."

GOD'S PERFECT TIMING—PART II

That small sliver of time we do get with our birth parents may be more than enough to bring peace and closure. It can be as simple as "Hello. I thought of you; you mattered to me. I am glad you found me." That may not sound like much, but for most of my clients, it's everything. When a birth parent has come to the end of his or her life, it's enough to be able to look in the eyes of their long-lost child to heal a lifetime of hurt. Even when one of my clients doesn't get the time to catch up on that lifetime, I consider the reunion a success. These are moments that go beyond words.

MAMA'S BOY

Mike Sommer, sixty-five, was a farm boy from Kansas who always used his words sparingly. His mother was thirty-four when she adopted him, and his dad was forty-four, and neither of them had the kind of health where they could run around and play with their son on the farm. Mike's father was a workaholic who toiled as a clerk for the railroad when he wasn't tilling the land. His mother, a homemaker and farmer's wife, was always getting sick. She'd had bouts with shingles, and a series of fifteen to twenty strokes over the years. She was the seventeenth patient in the United States to ever receive a new heart valve. The possibility that he could lose her had plagued him throughout his childhood.

"I was a mama's boy. She was my world," he told me.

Mike liked his solitude. He had no wish for siblings. When his mother wasn't spoiling him and baking fruit pies, he'd spend hours roaming the farm's land. His friends were the farmhands, his dog, and his vivid imagination.

"I would just wander around and play. I was used to it. If I was lonely, I didn't realize I was lonely," he recalled.

For the first ten years of his life, he could have been a boy version of Dorothy from *The Wizard of Oz*. But Mike's early existence was always clouded by potential tragedy. Any day, he knew, his frail mother could go. At nine, he was sent away to live with his grandmother for half a school year. His mom had an operation on her stomach, which didn't heal for months. She'd always been heavy, and this was causing complications. She was sent home to die, and again, Mike was sent away to Topeka to be with his grandmother, because his father was too busy to keep an eye on him. Yet somehow, she recovered.

ONLY CHILD

At some point in his early years—Mike isn't sure exactly when—he started asking why he didn't have any brothers or sisters. His parents seemed much older than his school friends' parents, so he figured something was up. They gently explained to him that they couldn't have any children of their own, so they'd adopted him and taken him home. They showed him a baby picture from the time he first joined the Sommer clan, surrounded by family members. There'd always been total acceptance of Mike as part of the family, and his situation felt normal to him. He wasn't angry or upset. The family drew him in. He was their boy.

"It just didn't seem like a big deal to me. Maybe I was a little too young to understand, but it was always the life I knew. Never in the course of living every day did I think about the fact that I was adopted."

THE BUSINESS OF LIFE

Life went on. His mother rallied from each illness and survived until the age of sixty-four, when Mike was thirty. Meanwhile, Mike, whose family members were devout Catholics, went to seminary school to study for the priesthood. An overwhelming interest in girls soon put that ambition to rest, so Mike joined the navy. When he was nineteen, he was stationed in Memphis, Tennessee, where he met and fell in love with a Baptist Southern belle. His future in-laws weren't happy about their daughter hooking up with a Yankee Catholic, so the young lovers eloped back in Kansas a year later. Happily married for the past forty-five years, Mike and his wife have two daughters and a granddaughter. He was so busy raising his own family, working long hours as a truck driver and then as a skilled factory worker, he barely gave his birth family a thought. Those blue-collar jobs took their toll. Besides, the idea of searching for his birth parents seemed a dishonor somehow to the mother and father who had raised him.

In 1973, he moved his family to Green Valley, just outside of Tucson, Arizona, to escape the cold. He took a job at the Raytheon factory—the same plant that made all the rockets fired in the Gulf wars. He worked in the chemical warehouse and disposal area—a very specialized job.

"I spent a lot of time wearing rubber suits," Mike recalled.

There was always a danger that his high level of exposure to lethal chemicals could lead to a work-related illness, like mesothelioma, so he decided to retire early, at fifty-five. He was convinced he was a ticking time bomb and that he would never live to a ripe old age. He wanted to relax and enjoy the time he had left.

BLANKS ON A MEDICAL FORM

Early retirement got him thinking. Every time he went to the doctor for a checkup, he had to fill out a form that asked about his parents' and grandparents' health history, and, of course, he knew nothing. He felt he owed it to his kids, and to their children, to learn about any possible genetic health issues. He went back to Kansas City and approached someone at the desk of the adoption records center. But Missouri is tough—the state keeps those records under lock and key. The clerk felt sorry for Mike and suggested he hire a state-licensed advocate to look at the records on his behalf. It would be the advocate's job to contact the woman named on the birth record. But if that person refused to speak to Mike, or if that person was dead, Mike would not be allowed to know either way.

"I thought, Well, shoot, why would I want to spend that money when this lady is probably dead by now?" Mike explained.

Instead of choosing that option, Mike tried to have a lawyer friend in Kansas sneak into the back door of the records center. They found out the documents really were locked away. It was a fortress in there. The more his attempts to find out were thwarted, the more he was determined to know. Pretty soon, it became an obsession. He went back to Kansas and got a copy of the non-identifying information. All he found out from those records was that his mother had graduated from high school and knew how to sew. He also learned that her parents were regular churchgoers. Her father was a farmer, and her mother was a homemaker who liked to play the clarinet. He learned that his birth mother had an uncle who was a corpsman in the navy, and another who owned a tavern. There were details of aunts, uncles, brothers, and sisters, but no names. To Mike it was just a list of useless facts, with lots of blacked-out text.

Mike's official birth certificate didn't offer many clues, either. It listed his adoptive parents' names, and the hospital that had issued the document, which was dated 1951, six years after Mike was born, leading him to believe that for his first few years he was probably his parents' foster child before being officially adopted. He never did find his adoption records. He tried the local Catholic agency that acted as the go-between for birth mothers and adoptive families, but he got nowhere. He even went to the little church where he'd been baptized, but those papers offered no clues, either—at least not to Mike.

HAZY MEMORIES

Mike remembered he had an older second cousin in his adoptive family who was more like an aunt and used to look after him and cuddle him as an infant. He searched for her, hoping she'd know some details surrounding his adoption. She told him she remembered that his birth mom was a big-band singer from California. But this cousin was in her nineties now, and he had no way of knowing whether her memory was playing tricks on her.

The more roadblocks he bumped against, the more he wanted to find out the truth. He hired a couple of private agencies to do searches. One woman the searchers found was actually younger than Mike. Another woman swore up and down she'd never had any children, in or out of wedlock. It meant thousands of dollars down the drain, money that a man on a fixed income could hardly afford.

"I felt like such a fool," he admitted.

Mike's wife, Patricia, could see his frustration. But she didn't want him to give up. "You need to get your mind happy about this," she told him. "Keep going."

All along, there'd been something missing in Mike's life, and his wife realized it more than he did. It was around this time that Mike came across an article in the Tucson paper about my old client Ann Haralambie. The article mentioned that Ann was a lawyer who connected adoptees with birth parents and that, after years of her own searching, I had found her birth mother for her. He tracked her down and asked if she could help him. She said she couldn't, as he had too little information to go on, but she knew someone who could, and she gave Mike my name and contact details.

"Pam's a miracle worker," she was kind enough to tell him. "I searched for my mother for more than thirty years, but it took her a matter of weeks to find her. If I were you, I'd call her now. There's no more time to waste."

Anne gave Mike my Web site information. Mike's a sweetheart, and although he was mistrustful of professional searchers, we were soon chatting away like old friends. He did his best to beat me down on my price. When I assured him it was no find, no fee, he took the leap. The information was paltry, but there were enough random pieces, I felt that I just might be able to connect them. It took me all of three days.

THE FAMILY HONOR

The first thing I had to do was locate his original birth name, and when I found it, I was relieved to see it was an uncommon Polish name: Matthew Majusiak. The rest fell into place pretty quickly. His mother's name was Lucy Majusiak, the daughter of strict old-world Catholics from Poland. Lucy was twenty-eight, jobless at the time, and living with her parents. It was toward the end of World War II, and there weren't too many eligible men around to marry a nice girl like Lucy, but she met and fell in love with an older man and they had a passionate love affair. He was a World War I veteran and a factory worker who made parachutes for the war effort. When she found out she was pregnant, she went to his house to tell him, hoping he'd do the right thing and marry her. She knocked on the door and a woman answered; it was his wife, who was surrounded by the philandering man's five children. Lucy'd had no idea he was married, and she wasn't about to drop a bombshell on the woman and ruin her life, so she made up some excuse for the visit, turned around, and walked away. She cut off all contact and never discussed him again. It wasn't clear why she'd never been to his home before, or where they'd managed to find a place for their secret trysts.

When she told her family, there was no question she had to give the baby up. In their eyes, she was a sinner, and this was a big slap in the face to a devout Catholic family hell-bent on making it through the gates of Heaven. As far as they were concerned, their family honor came before Lucy's wish to keep the child. They had a son in the priesthood, and they were worried that the scandal of a child born out of wedlock would jeopardize his chances of being ordained. All of the family's ambitions revolved around their son. They'd lived in a mining town near Hazelton, Pennsylvania, and came from a long line of coal miners and bakers in the region. But when the favorite son was assigned to Henry, South Dakota, they picked up and moved the whole family so they could be near him. They were halfway across the country and in the middle of nowhere, cut off from their extended family and forced to start their lives over from scratch, but they were such devout Catholics that it didn't matter. They remade themselves into farmers, and there the family stayed.

OUT OF THE WAY

Lucy was distraught over the thought of giving up her unborn child. But like any good girl who was terrified of her father, she did as she was told. They banished her to a shelter for unwed mothers in Kansas City, long before there was any danger of her pregnancy showing. While she was safely out of the way, she had to work to pay for her own room and board by sewing uniforms for soldiers. That's how Mike ended up a farm boy in Kansas.

Two years later, Lucy married and became Mrs. Strophus and, about a year after that, she gave birth to her second son, Francis.

Of course, these were details Mike would eventually have to explore for himself. I could only guess at some of the circumstances. From what I could piece together, his birth mother's story was like so many other stories of birth mothers from those days. When they gave up a child for adoption, it wasn't really their choice. Their families were usually hard on them. It was their mistake, and they would have to suffer the consequences.

LINING UP THE PIECES

When I called Mike to tell him I'd found his birth family, he was stunned. It seemed too good to be true, and he was beginning to think he was being scammed again. I went through the list of relatives mentioned on the nonidentifying records, giving him names and past known addresses for all of them. Everything had been checked and cross-checked. When he was convinced this was real, I told him he had a half brother. I'd spoken with a female cousin to make sure the names lined up before I passed on the numbers of Mike's brother, Francis, and his cousin, Marie. These were the right people. There could be no doubt. But, as often happens when a search suddenly gets real, he balked.

"Mike, you need to call them," I said.

"I can't call these people and say, 'Ring, ring, guess who I am.' I wouldn't want to get that phone call."

"Michael, God has put this in front of you for a reason, whether they are good results or bad. This is what you have been wanting all along."

"Would you do it for me?" he asked.

I gave Marie the heads-up that he would be in touch, and she was more than excited to talk to him. Mike then reached out to Marie to find out how her cousin, his brother, would react to the news. She assured him that Francis was a nice guy and would probably be okay with it. While he was on the phone, he e-mailed a picture of himself, and Marie told him he looked exactly like his mother.

"I do?" he said

"Yep, no doubt about it. You are related to us," Marie assured him.

Then Marie sent a picture of Francis, and Mike found the resemblance shocking. Any uncertainty that this was the right family was erased. When he finally worked up the courage to call his brother, Francis told him he'd been expecting his call. Then he told him a story.

OUT OF THE BLUE

Two years earlier, Lucy had wanted to do some shopping so Francis drove his mother to Watertown—the big city in the area, with a population of 100,000. Out of nowhere, as they were driving, Lucy blurted out, "Hey, guess what. You have a brother!"

Francis was so surprised, he nearly veered off the road. There was no reason for her to bring this up. He could only imagine that something in the passing landscape had triggered an old memory. As they continued to drive, they talked about what had happened to Lucy and how she came to give Mike up. By then, her memory was faulty. She kept recalling his place of birth as St. Louis instead of Kansas, probably because she'd taken a trip there around the same time. But Lucy was very clear about one thing: Francis should try to find his brother if he could. The problem was, he had no idea where to begin, so he just let the information lie there in the back of his mind.

"So you see, Mike," Francis informed him, "I'm not completely shocked to hear from you."

They chatted a little more. Francis briefed him on the state of Lucy's health, which was fragile, and he told him a few things about what their mom was like. The brothers' lives were similar in many ways. Francis had also been raised on a farm as an only child, and was doted on by his mother. Like Mike, Francis was spoiled. His mom enjoyed baking lots of fruit pies and cooking hearty, wholesome meals for the family. She loved nothing more than to get out into the fields and do all the chores on their eight-hundred-acre farm. She was always happy and easygoing, even though the family had been through many hardships.

When Francis was seventeen, his father passed away. Lucy and Francis were left to run the farm on their own, with help from a loyal farmhand. Lucy never complained, and she had no problem getting her hands dirty, not that she had a choice.

There were several occasions when hardships hit and the family had to start from scratch, literally. A tornado once demolished the property and they had to completely rebuild their home. Until just a few years earlier, Lucy stayed on at the farmhouse, living with Francis and his wife and helping to care for their kids. The arrangement worked out well. Francis took a job in town as a factory worker and his wife worked as a nurse. They needed Lucy's help. But as the years wore on, it became clear that Lucy could no longer be left by herself. She'd forget to turn off the stove, and it was getting harder for her to move around and climb the stairs on her own. They had no choice but to put her into an assisted-living facility.

NOW OR NEVER

Mike also learned that Lucy, who by now was ninety-three, suffered from a heart condition. She'd just been moved to hospice care at the nursing home because she had not been eating well, and she had a "do not resuscitate" order. A couple of recent minor blips with her heart made Mike nervous that time was running out, so he asked Francis if it would be okay for him to visit. Francis said he'd talk to Lucy and get back to him. The next day, he called Mike back and said that not only would she be willing to see him, she was looking forward to it.

Three weeks later, Mike and his wife were on a plane to Sioux Falls, where the nearest airport was located. They had a hotel room reserved near the tiny town where Francis lived, about one hundred miles away. As soon as Mike deplaned, he called to tell Francis they were on their way. When Mike pulled up to the front of the area's only decent hotel, he saw a burly man with facial features similar to his own; he was looking anxious. As soon as Mike stepped out of the car, his younger brother enveloped him in a huge bear hug.

The family could not have been more welcoming. Mike's newfound aunts, uncles, and cousins owned a flower shop in Watertown, and when Mike and his wife got to their hotel room, it was filled with fresh flowers. Mike asked if he could take some flowers to Lucy, and his cousin arranged for a huge bouquet. Then he headed to the nursing home, accompanied by his wife and Francis. His brother introduced him as they walked into the hospice ward, then politely excused himself so they could have some privacy. Lucy was propped up on pillows, frail and gaunt-looking, but alert and expectant. Mike walked in with his wife and handed his mother the flowers. She set them aside as he leaned over her bed; then she held the sixty-four-year-old man's wrinkled face in her hands and cooed, "My baby boy! My baby boy!"

She knew exactly who he was. Mike's wife, who knew more than he did how much this reunion meant to him, was crying. Mike sat beside Lucy's bed and started asking the usual questions: "How did the adoption happen?" "Why was I given up?" "Who was my birth father?" The information was hard to piece together because Lucy's speech was impaired. She had only a few teeth left, part of her nose was missing from skin cancer, and she was suffering from mild dementia. She was also hard-of-hearing, so words were slow for her to process and difficult to understand. Mike had to ask her to repeat things, and he didn't want to push it too far. Mostly, they just held hands and smiled at each other. It was enough for now that they could be together. But what he did learn was that her family had made her suffer for having a child out of wedlock. She'd never wanted to give him up, and she'd never forgotten about him. "I thought of you often," she told him. She'd hoped one day he'd find her, and she was overjoyed that he finally had.

"I wasn't mad. I was just glad to see her. Back then, when you didn't have a job or a place to go, you did what your dad told you to do. She didn't have a choice," Mike later told me.

MY OTHER SON

The following morning, Mike visited Lucy again. By then, the rumor mill had started buzzing. When a nurse came into Lucy's room and saw the flowers, she asked, "Who brought you all those pretty flowers?"

"My son brought them," Lucy replied.

"What? Francis doesn't do flowers! He's not that kind of guy."

"No! My other son!"

The nurses at the home were so happy for Lucy, they arranged for a big family reunion dinner at the local Elks' Club. It seemed like half the town of Henry showed up to meet Mike and Patricia, with aunts, cousins, second cousins, nieces, and nephews all in attendance, seated around a huge U-shaped table. The family treated him like one of their own. He made an instant connection with his aunt Olga, Lucy's sister-in-law, a vigorous ninety-year-old woman who still manages the family flower shop where Mike got his bouquet.

"You are so much like her," she told him. "It's hard to believe you grew up so far away from her. It seems like you should have been together."

Olga insisted he call her "Aunt Olga," just like all the other "children" over sixty in the family. If he didn't, she said she'd consider him a disrespectful youngster and there'd be hell to pay.

"She was funnier than a hat trick. Matter of fact, I kept calling her Olga just to wind her up!" Mike told me.

Each member of the family lined up to meet him and hear the story of how he'd found Lucy. There were toasts, hugs, and kisses all around. Mike felt like a celebrity. At birth-family reunions, there's almost always someone in the extended family who is disbelieving and endlessly questions the searcher. But when I asked Mike how it went, he told me it was one of the most joyful experiences he'd ever had. "I don't know how I would have reacted if the tables had been turned. I guess I would have been suspicious, but evidently these people were a lot nicer than I am," Mike said.

TWO PEAS

Mike stuck around for a few more days. He used the time to get to know his brother, Francis, who is a lot like him, and not just in terms of looks. Mike has a lumbering gait, where, according to him "my arms swing kind of funny," and Francis does, too. They're both kind and gentle men who are soft-spoken and deliberate in the way they speak. They both have a dry sense of humor that not everybody gets. "But when I tell a joke, Francis is right there with me," says Mike. The brothers both like to work hard and enjoy the outdoors.

"It's freaky. The way we eat. The way we talk. We are so similar," Mike told me.

It was almost as if they'd been raised together, Mike explained. As kids, they were each pretty happy with their "only child" status, but on their first chance to sit down and really talk, there was a lot of discussion about what life would have been like if they'd grown up under the same roof. There were definite advantages to growing up the way they had, but at times they'd found themselves wishing for a brother or a sister.

"Not that I would have wanted to grow up in South Dakota," Mike joked.

It was late summer when Mike made his first visit, and he hatched plans with Francis to return for another visit before the winter set in, to make the most of the time he had left with his birth mother. Before Mike left, Francis gave him a list of every family member's name and contact details so that he could stay in the loop and fully participate in the lives of his newfound extended family. He also gave Mike his mother's old address book, hoping it would help give him more clues about Lucy's past, and who his birth father was. The information was sketchy and not entirely accurate, but he thinks he may have located the town where he lived. He'd be long dead by now, as he was much older than Lucy, and Mike is convinced his birth father's side of the family knows nothing of his existence.

He's reluctant to pick at that wound, but he would like to know a little more about his family's health history. His one last hope for finding his birth father was to contact Lucy's only surviving sibling, a ninety-five-year-old nun still living in Pennsylvania. On Mike's behalf, Francis contacted her, but the nun claimed no knowledge of Lucy's having had a child out of wedlock and swore it wasn't possible. Mike put that down to dementia or denial. Among her immediate family, Lucy's story simply didn't fit the "good Catholic" profile.

WIPED CLEAN

It's as if that whole episode in her life was erased from the family archives. There weren't even any pictures of Lucy taken around the time Mike was born. His cousins dug up colorized pictures of his mother from when she was a teenager, out snowshoeing in the Pennsylvania hills. She liked to do all the things Mike enjoyed, like hiking in the great outdoors. She was fresh-faced, hearty, and cheerful.

"If you pulled her hair back, she could have been me at that age. Our faces were identical," Mike told me.

Not until she was married would she pose for the cameras again. There were plenty of pictures of the rest of the family, but during those lost years of grief after she gave up her baby boy, it was as if she didn't exist.

But Mike had no intention of bringing up any painful topics

directly with Lucy. Their time together was too precious. He figured if there was something he needed to know, she'd find a way of telling him when she was ready. Mike stopped by the nursing home once more to visit Lucy. She didn't want to let him go. She kept pulling him closer and stroking his face, as if she wanted to make sure he was real. Lucy couldn't get enough of her long-lost son. Then she fixed her eyes on a gold crucifix he was wearing, and beamed. If she could just borrow it for a while, she told him then he'd have to come back and see her again.

"I couldn't resist her. She talked me out of it!" he said.

They hugged and said their good-byes, and when Mike got home, he tried calling her at the nursing home, but communication was difficult. Instead, he wrote letters, which she asked the nursing staff to read to her over and over again.

Two weeks later, Lucy died. Mike's next visit to the Mount Rushmore state was for his birth mother's funeral. Members of the Majusiak clan flew in from all over the country. He could hear the whispers of speculation among relatives and family friends who'd missed the news of his last visit. Francis had mentioned Mike as Lucy's other son in the local paper's obituary, but the out-of-towners had no idea who this stranger was in the family's pew at the church. At the reception after the funeral, dozens of people came up to greet him.

"It was poor Lucy's burial day, but I was the center of attention," Mike recalled.

Before she was put in the ground, Francis gave the gold cross back to Mike. Knowing that Lucy wore it in her final days, he never takes it off. "I really treasure it now," he told me.

The event of their mother's passing drew the brothers even closer together. Mike has gained a brother and a huge family of cousins, aunts, uncles, nieces, and nephews he never had. The February following their mother's death, Mike invited Francis and his wife, Shelly, to visit Tucson, and he showed them the sights. They speak on the phone at least a couple of times a month and e-mail almost daily.

"I am getting to know a man I really, really like," Mike said.

Francis has a son, two daughters, and five grandchildren, and they all call Mike and his wife "Uncle Mike" and "Aunt Pat." They write regularly to tell them how much they are missed. Mike's planning to take his wife and three daughters for a summer visit to Henry, South Dakota. At first, his daughters were concerned he'd be hurt by his search for his birth family, but now they are thrilled.

A SPECIAL PLACE

Mike still doesn't think of Lucy as his mother. The woman who raised him owns that title. But, as he puts it, "She occupies a particular niche in my heart. I appreciate her strength in giving me away. It took a lot of courage."

After the funeral, he saw the graves of Lucy's parents—his grandparents—and he didn't look too kindly on them. The religious bigotry they exhibited was something the former seminary student had witnessed far too often. It was part of the reason he had taken a step back from the Catholic Church. His grandparents could have kept him in the family and raised him, but instead they forced his mother to choose between keeping her baby or being tossed into the streets, with nowhere to go. As far as Mike is concerned, putting a young woman in that position for the sake of faith was unforgivable. "They allowed religion to get in the way of my birth mother's happiness," he said.

But he is grateful to his grandparents for their longevity genes. That may be one reason why he's still alive despite all the chemical hazards of his former occupation. That may also be why his birth mother survived long enough to meet him. Or maybe it was all part of God's plan. As sad as he was to lose Lucy so soon after meeting her, his reunion fell into place so perfectly, it restored Mike's faith just a little bit. It gave Lucy the closure she needed to pass in peace, and it gave Mike the answers he needed to live in peace.

"In my heart, I know she was waiting for me," he explained.

Mike and Owen found their birth mothers just in time. Both reunions were joyful, despite the loss and sorrow that inevitably follow when a birth parent is well into her eighth or ninth decade. But even when people don't find one another in time, there's a reason. It's part of a plan. I see it all the time. Death can spare us from the pain of a revelation we don't want, and open the door to answers that we truly need.

The Lesson: God Has Perfect Timing

When a reunion happens, it tends to happen at the right time and for the right reason. I can think of hundreds of cases where, if the birth parent had been found earlier, the connection could have gone horribly wrong. Every time I work a case, I say a little prayer and ask God if it's meant to happen. I ask Him to give me the wisdom to solve the search, but only if it's His will.

Of course, as perfect as God's timing may be, you have to help yourself along the way. How sad would it have been if Mike and Owen had never had the opportunity to say thank you and good-bye to the sweet and long-suffering women who had given them life? I have heard countless times from my clients that they are hesitant to search, for fear of intruding on their birth parents' lives. In response, I ask the question, "How will you ever know unless you try?" The most important part of searching is to make sure you do it in a respectful and confidential manner. Most people are happy to have their answers and, at a minimum, much-needed closure.

If you don't make that connection, you might always be left with unanswered questions. The what-ifs might follow you around for a lifetime. You will never get to hold the hand of your birth mother and look into the eyes that will tell you everything you ever needed to know. So don't be afraid. Despite what happened in my own search, I'd do it all over again. The search is worth the risk.

CHAPTER THIRTEEN

I'm Okay

• ◆ •

I did hear from Priscilla, my birth mother, again. It seems no one was surprised by this but me. She'd been circling around me, putting feelers out through Vinnie and my sisters, for months. But nothing had prepared me for her phone call. This time, I recognized her phone number. I took a deep breath and picked up.

"Hello, Pamela, this is Priscilla."

"Oh. What can I do for you?"

My guard was up. I supposed the promos for my show on OWN, the Oprah Winfrey Network, and various press notices she'd read about me on the Internet, had made her take a second look at the daughter she'd always claimed she didn't want to know. Not that my successes or failures should matter. As far as I was concerned, she should have wanted to know me for who I am, not what I am or what I could do for her. I figured I knew what was coming next.

"It's about your sister, Diana," Priscilla said.

"I thought you said she wasn't my sister."

"Yes, your sister. She's in trouble. Her boyfriend is beating her up and she needs to move out. Can you help her with money or furniture?"

"Priscilla, of course I'll help her in any way I can."

Frankly, I just wanted to get her off the phone. I didn't really believe that Priscilla was asking on behalf of Diana. I was sure that if Diana were in trouble, she'd reach out to me directly. It seemed more like a ploy, as if Priscilla was using Diana to open up the dialogue with me for what she hoped would be her own eventual financial gain.

"Please, whatever you can do. Her boyfriend's a drug addict and he beats her. I know what that's like. I've been in a similar situation. She's a good girl. She needs help."

"If that's true, Priscilla, then you deserve help, too."

I could hear that she was starting to cry.

"I am getting what I deserve," she said.

In that moment, I realized something. Priscilla's rejection of me when I first reached out to her all those years ago had nothing to do with who I was. A birth parent's rejection of the one who is searching is never really about how she feels about the child she gave up. This was something I'd always told my clients, but never myself. That rejection is not personal. It's about the guilt, fear, or denial of something that's too painful to remember or acknowledge.

I had tried to steamroll into my birth mother's life and she'd put up a concrete wall. Now I know where I get some of my fierce tenacity. Like Priscilla, I can be tough when I feel like I'm being crossed. Threaten me or my family and I turn into a tiger. I can also be blunt to a fault. If someone pisses me off, I have no problem speaking my mind. But the loving environment in which I was raised has also taught me compassion.

I have no regrets about reaching out to Priscilla the way I did. I am glad I found Vinnie and my sisters. Despite the pain and disappointment of reunions that fell short and relationships that faltered, I've learned so much about who I am. Most of all, it has taught me to appreciate the family that raised me, and for that, I can't thank Priscilla enough. She gave birth to me when she didn't have to, and she struggled with the decision to give me up for adoption so that I could have a better life. It was an unselfish and loving act, no matter what has happened between us since. I'm not angry with my birth mother. The pain she caused me is over, and from the bottom of my heart, I wish her well. I know her life has been hard, and she's entitled to a little peace and happiness in this lifetime.

Priscilla, I want you to know that I'm okay. And I hope you're okay, too.

About the Author

• • •

Run–DMC's Darryl McDaniels calls Pamela Slaton "my PI for the adopted guy." Oprah Winfrey and her network executives were so impressed with her story and passion for her work that they gave Pam a prime-time show on the Oprah Winfrey Network, which launched in February 2011. And she's had plenty of stories to tell. Over the past fifteen years, the author has successfully reunited close to three thousand adoptees with their birth parents, and she has done so against the most impossible odds.

It takes a special breed to carry out the kind of delicate research work needed to find these missing people. Pamela combines resourcefulness, compassion, and dogged determination to help her clients realize their lifelong dreams. Because she is a genealogist specializing in missing persons, they come to her when all other avenues have failed.

Even private investigators and law-enforcement personnel seek her out to find their birth parents because they know they lack her amazing trace skills. These detectives aren't typically equipped to find people without very precise information. Most of Pam's clients have no first name, date of birth, or place of birth for the birth mother. The facts she works with are tiny and disparate.

"My talent lies in having the ability to find old records and combine them with contemporary data," says Pam. Of course, there's much more to it than that. This is a woman who knows how to follow a hunch all the way to the end.

Family has always been Pam's defining passion—whether it's her own or her clients'. This loving wife and proud mother of two young men—a seventeen-year-old and a twenty-two-year-old—carries out her life-changing work from her home in suburban New Jersey, vacuuming and dusting between phone calls and data downloads. She works weekends and well into the night, never stopping until she's nailed a lead. She refuses to give up, because reconnecting lost loved ones isn't just work for Pam; it's personal.

She discovered who her own birth parents were more than a decade ago. The search for her birth mother ended badly, but as she endeavored to piece together those shattered hopes, she came to discover her true vocation as a searcher. When she started on her quest, there were scant services available to those looking for clues. Pam began volunteering her services to local adoptee support groups and was eventually hired as the New York contact for a major adoption-finder agency.

She soon became disenchanted with the agency's ethics and decided to strike out on her own with a "no-find, no-fee" payment policy to help reestablish trust between clients and professional searchers.

Her track record has been so stellar that she's caught the attention of several print and media outlets, including the *New York Times*, *Newsday*, and the *Boston Globe*. Pam's a sought-after television personality who's been featured on Fox's *Mike and Juliet;* ABC's *Nightline,* with a story that followed one woman's search for her birth parents from beginning to end; and on VH1, in *My Adoption Journey,* an Emmy-winning documentary about DMC's quest for his birth parents. More recently, in February 2010, Pam appeared on *Oprah,* where she helped a mother search for the baby girl she was forced to give up for adoption when she was just fifteen.

A native New Yorker who was born in the Bronx and raised in Queens, Pam has a warmth and humor that come across loud and clear on these television appearances. She keeps it real. She doesn't raise expectations. And yet she never says it can't be done. "I've witnessed the most impossible cases come together. What is meant to happen will happen as long as you are persistent," she says.

This no-nonsense, direct approach, combined with her genuine understanding and concern for those who seek, are what prompted Oprah to give Pam her own show, *Searching for . . .*

Pam's emotionally invested in her work because she has walked in the shoes of every one of her clients. She knows firsthand the anxiety and fear they go through when they undertake the search, and she views herself as part of their support system. She takes each client under her wing and prepares them for a gamut of emotions. Even the most joyous reunions can be complicated. Searching takes mental preparation and the self-assurance that you can accept any outcome.

Pam's often asked why she would involve herself in this type of work after the pain and fallout of her own disastrous reunion. Her answer is simple: "I love what I do. It gives me great joy to witness my clients having the opportunity to finally have closure after years of searching. Each successful reunion helps heal a little piece of my heart."

Acknowledgments

◆ ◆ ◆

My heartfelt thanks to the following people:

My mom and dad for their undying love and inspiration to follow my dreams.

My brother for showing me what true courage means.

My husband, Mike, who completes me. He has shown me that people can be trusted and that I am worth loving. He also taught me not to take myself so seriously.

My sons, Ron and Mikey, of whom I am incredibly proud, and who I love more than I could have ever imagined. They are my heart and soul.

My sister, Kathy, who makes me laugh more than anyone I know. She makes me aware of how amazing shared DNA can be. It is a very powerful thing.

My mother-in-law, Joan, who has taken over for Mike and me when we have to travel for work. I'm so grateful to know that our kids, and Jake the dog, are in such safe hands.

Special acknowledgment to:

Katherine Boros

Wendy Freund

Sheila Jaffe

Cathy Konrad

Stuart Krasnow

Darryl McDaniels

Ginger Simpson

Thank you so much to all of my clients who have entrusted me to help them navigate the waters of search and reunion. I would never have experienced the many blessings of my life without you. More important, you have allowed me to bear witness to some of the most incredible moments of my life, and it has restored the many broken pieces of my heart. You have been gracious in allowing me to share your stories, and I hope that I have made you proud.

And I am eternally grateful to Oprah Winfrey, for giving me the opportunity of a lifetime.

Finally, thank you, Samantha "Sammy" Marshall for understanding my vision for this book and the work that I so love. You made writing this book a wonderful experience.